Research your Therapy

- analyze your results -

and Publish

Examples in JASP, a free and user friendly analysis tool

Gordon Emmerson, PhD

Old Golden Point Press

Blackwood, Victoria: Australia

ISBN-10: 0992499569

ISBN-13: 978-0992499563

> More good research is needed,
> and too often those who have the will and the skills
> to do research
> do not have the technical knowledge to complete it.

This book is not written for statisticians.

It is written for therapists who have techniques they want to share.

Resource Therapy

This book is to encourage research and publication in Resource Therapy, but the skills presented here can be applied to conduct research on any therapeutic orientation.

The datasets used are freely downloadable for practice, as they were created for illustration, and were not collected from actual research participants.

Thank you to my son Daniel

His consistent support has
given me a foundation to both enjoy and to work.

Contents

Statisitical Notations

Name	Notation	Page
Mean	M	15
Entire # in a sample	N	32
# in subgroup of a sample	n	32
Probability of error	p	34
Standard Deviation	SD	41
Eta^2	η^2	39
Partial eta^2	η^2_p	70
Correlation	r	52
Coefficient of determination	r^2	39
Variance explained in a regression	R^2	39
t value	t	62
F value	F	67

Chapter 1: Introduction

Chapter 1 explains how this book is laid out and what you can expect to learn from it. It is good to get an overview of what you are going to learn, so everything you read has a context in a bigger picture. This book has information about

1) how to design research,

2) how to analyze research findings,

3) how to report those findings, and

4) how to structure a research article.

It also includes information about how to get through the publishing process.

You are here for a good reason. You have something you want to research and share with the world. Publishing will not only help other therapists and their clients, it will also be positive for your career.

This book is not written for statisticians. It is written for therapists who have good techniques that they want to share. If you keep in mind, while reading, some research you would like to do, that will make understanding easier and more interesting.

Enough is covered here to do and write good research. This book is written in a 'need to know', step by step fashion so you can better understand exactly how to go about your research.

Each chapter will now be briefly summarized to give you an overall context as you read.

Chapter 2: What makes a research article good?

Chapter 2 discusses the components of a research article. Getting an idea of the final product is important in learning each step. You would not start building a house without seeing an image of what you will have when you finish. When you write an article, you might as well write it in a way that is compelling to the reader, in a way that truly transmits the information you want understood. Chapter 2 gives some ideas about how to make that happen.

Chapter 3: Research design

Chapter 3 contains information that is key to do a research study. It is possible to get help with the statistical analysis, but unless you have designed your research project in the right way you will never be able to say your therapy or your technique helped clients. Chapter 3 is about how to design research. It includes information that allows you to gain a conceptual understanding of what is needed for good research. If you learn the concept of 'why' something works you remember it much better than if you just do rote learning. The design chapter provides you with a selection of research designs that you can choose from when you do your project.

Chapter 4: Statistical analysis

Don't run away. Chapter 4 presents what you need to know about analyzing your findings. It includes how to get a free statistical package, JASP, and it goes through the step by step process of conducting each analysis. It includes exactly what to report from the analysis and it gives an example for each analysis of a results paragraph. This chapter only includes common analyses that are used in researching therapies. To keep it simple and straightforward, these examples and illustrations of reports are for comparing only two groups. Most therapy research compares only two groups. Should you want to compare more than two groups, examples are given in the appendices. This analysis chapter includes how to code your data, how to get it into the statistical program, how to run your procedure, and how to report it.

Chapter 5: The publishing process

Chapter 5 contains information about the publishing process. Editors have expectations about what they want to see, and about the formatting and the presentation. Before you begin writing your article, you will want to be aware of the roadmap that needs to be followed to get to your destination, publication. You would not drive to a new location, without a GPS, unless you had a good idea about how to get there. The publishing process is your roadmap. Become familiar with it and your journey will be one without detours. At least, one with fewer detours. An Australian Prime Minister, Malcolm Frasier, once said, "Life wasn't meant to be easy." While the rewards are great and worthwhile, this can sometimes be an apt quote in relation to the publishing process. Even more reason to keep your publishing process map close.

Chapter 6: Writing your article

Chapter 6 is where all that has been learned in this book comes together into writing an article. An illustrative article is written based on the data used in the analysis section of this book. This section should be read with an understanding of what has been learned in the preceding chapters. To better solidify your learning, read each part of the article thinking about how it responds to what is required. For example, when you read the methodology section of the article, think about how the example satisfies the publishing requirements for a methodology section.

A message throughout this book is the value of a research design that allows the writer to say that the therapy 'caused' a change for the clients. Notice the value of being able to use this kind of 'causal' language in this sample article.

Chapter 7: Non-experimental and non-research articles

Chapter 7 is about writing non-research articles. The central focus of this book is for conducting research and publishing it. Research defines the efficacy of a therapy or a technique, and it is research articles that promote the utility of a therapy. An 'intervention of choice' is rightfully based on research.

Non-research articles refer to research articles. They can relate to a theory, or they can inform the reader about a technique. These are important articles, and even though they are not the focus of this book, you may also be interested in writing articles of this type. Therefore, I have included a chapter about how non-research articles can be structured.

Chapter 8: How to build a career

The first reason to do research is to contribute. It is a good feeling to do something that others find interesting and useful, especially when it can change lives for the better. A supplemental benefit to conducting and publishing research is the impact it has on the researcher's career. This chapter is about this aspect of publishing and about how to gain the most benefit from the hard work you do in your research.

Before you start

Before you know something, it can seem difficult. Afterward, it seems less complex and more obvious. It would be very normal for you to feel a bit over-awed about research and analysis. If you take your time with each chapter and allow yourself to absorb what is being said at your own pace, you will learn more easily.

Chapter 2: What makes a research article good?

There is both beauty in utility, and utility in beauty. For example, it is wonderful that John Kennedy was a man of substance, and his substantive words were understood, because he said them eloquently. This chapter shines a light on writing to be heard, on writing eloquently. That is our purpose. It shows where we are going.

A good research article moves from

1. general (introduce the topic to draw the reader in),

2. to specific (tell about what you did and what was learned),

3. to general (explain the importance of the research).

A good research article is written in a way that tells a story. We want readers to read and understand our research. The reader should want to read further. What is read should be clear. Here is how to write an article professionally, like telling a story.

Abstract

An abstract should be a summary of the article in about 150 words. You will need to check the requirements of the journal where you are sending your article to learn precisely how long your abstract needs to be. It is often good to include key words in the abstract to help those searching for research findings to find your article. This will help with the number of times your article is read and referenced.

The reader of an abstract should be able to learn something about the results of the study. The abstract does more than tell what was studied, it provides a glimpse of the major findings. Even though it comes at the beginning of an article, it is normally the last part of a report that is written. It would be hard to summarize a report before it is written.

Introduction

A good article has a short introduction that draws the reader into the topic. General statements about the importance of the topic help draw the reader in, leading to precisely what is being studied. The purpose of the introduction is both to define the topic and to promote interest.

Literature Review

Once the subject has been defined, the reader should learn who was the first to study this topic, and learn how findings in this area have progressed to the present day. At the end of this review a statement should be made regarding what we do not know. At this point, the reader has progressed from becoming interested in the topic, to hearing the story of what has been discovered. Like the reader in any story, your reader will want to discover what comes next. There is an interest in learning about the next finding, your finding. That desire to know the next finding makes it easier for the impact of your study to be understood and remembered. After you have captured and developed attention, you present your research aim, and research hypothesis.

Methodology

The methodology section tells the reader exactly how the research was carried out, including how participants were accessed, and the exact steps of the study. It is normally a short section, but it should be detailed enough to allow a further researcher to replicate the study. This section is not difficult to write, as it is quite straightforward. If scales were used in the study, such as a clinical depression inventory, they should be presented along with any reliability and validity information they came with. At the end of this section, the reader will understand exactly how the research hypothesis was tested and will be interested in learning about the findings.

Results

The results section is often very short. Each results paragraph should include four things, 1) what was being investigated, 2) what statistic was used, 3) what the finding was, and 4) what the finding means. No elaboration on the finding should be in the results section, as that will be in the discussion section, but the reader should

> Mean (M): The arithmetic average. The mean of 4, 7, and 5 is $(4+6+5)/3$ or 5

be able to read a results paragraph and gain an understanding about what was discovered. At the end of the results section the reader will know the findings that answer the research question, and will be ready to hear more about the greater meaning of those findings.

Discussion

It is in the discussion section that your voice, as the researcher, can really come out. Here you can take findings from the results section and explain them. The findings can be compared to what other people have found in the past. Sometimes they confirm previous findings, and sometimes they refute them. They may provide totally new results. You can talk about the meaning of the results, and you may want to give recommendations. If there are any limitations they can be discussed, and a call for further research can be made. Your article should end with a broad statement relating to the greater meaning of the findings.

At this point the story of your research will have been told, from introducing the topic and making it interesting, to leading the reader through what has been discovered in the past to what needed to be discovered. Your reader was then told how the study was conducted, what the findings were, and was finally told the greater meaning of the findings. When a research article is presented in this way, it is better heard and has a better chance of advancing change.

We can now see exactly where research findings fit into the published work. While the framing of the findings is very important, it is ultimately important to have findings based on well-structured research. Some research designs allow you to say that your intervention caused change, and some do not. Research takes time and it is wise to use that time in a way that provides compelling results. It is nice to be proud of the research you do, rather than wish you had done it in a different way. The following section will provide information about the nature and importance of doing experimental research, when possible.

Chapter 3: Research design

Non-research articles

There are many non-causal research articles about a therapy or a therapeutic intervention that describe how or why a therapy works, or describe how to conduct an intervention. The techniques for writing theory and practice articles are included in Chapter 7: Non-experimental and non-research articles. These are important articles but they fall short of scientifically demonstrating the effectiveness of a therapy, or of an intervention. The core focus of this book is on how to do 'Causal Research' to demonstrate efficacy. Causal research needs to be planned appropriately to follow reasoned procedures. It is not difficult to conduct when these procedures are known and understood.

Research design and causal research

Research design is very important when researching a therapy, especially when we want to give the reader enough evidence to understand the value of the therapy or intervention. It is the design of the research that allows the researcher to say the therapy resulted in a change. Research that is designed to do this is called causal research. Following a causal research study, the researcher can say it was the therapy that caused the improvement, rather than some other factor.

The three types of research design

1. Non-experimental (sometimes called pre-experimental): These designs can demonstrate a significant difference between a pre-test and a post-test, or between two groups, but they cannot attribute that difference to the therapy.

2. Quasi-experimental: These designs eliminate almost all possible reasons for an improvement other than the therapy. Any other cause may be eliminated through a reasoned explanation.
3. Experimental: These designs incorporate a random assignment of participants to treatment groups (either to treatment and control groups, or to varied treatment groups). These designs pinpoint the therapy as the reason for an improvement. Experimental designs are sometimes referred to as Gold Standard Research.

Non-experimental designs

One group pre-post design

The most common non-experimental design is the (one group) pre-post design. That means there was a test both before (pre) and after (post) a treatment. A single group is given a test before the treatment, then given the same test again after the treatment. A positive change is an indication that the treatment may have helped. "May have" is all that can be said, following a pre-post design. Any change 'may have' been due to the treatment, or it 'may have' been due to any of several other reasons.

What else may have caused the change?

Campbell and Stanley (2015) clearly defined reasons the pre-post design cannot be considered causal research. Using their terminology, here are those reasons. You will see that adding a control group to a research design is very important when we want to be able to say that our treatment causes a change.

Maturation

Research participants naturally change over time. Any natural change that affects what is being studied is called Maturation. For example, persons with depression will naturally become less depressed as the seasons move from winter to spring. Also, a natural healing will often occur when a person suffers from a disorder. When the reader of research cannot tell if a change is due to the treatment or to another factor, such as Maturation, then the researcher cannot claim that the treatment caused the change.

Maturation can even refer to a natural change that occurs that moves the participant to a worse condition. For example, if the research started in summer and continued into the colder months the participants would naturally become more depressed, so Maturation would mask the effectiveness of the treatment.

Preventing Maturation from being a problem in research

When a control group is added to the design, then both the treatment and control groups will be exposed to the same natural changes. If there are not pre-existing differences between the control and the treatment groups that cloud the results, then any difference between the treatment and control groups in the post-test can be attributed to the treatment.

History

History is the term for an unplanned event that could impact on the results of your research. For example, if we are studying depression and a new drug comes out and participants take that drug, this could impact on depression levels and mask the researcher's ability to see the value of the therapy. Likewise, a positive or negative event in the news could raise or lower the depression levels of participants. If a sporting team related to the area of your study wins a major championship, depression levels might lower, or if a tragedy is reported in the news, depression levels might rise.

Preventing History from being a problem in research

When a control group is added to the design, then both the treatment and control groups will be exposed to the same historic events. If there are not pre-existing differences between the control and the treatment groups that cloud the results, then any difference between the treatment and control groups in the post-test can be attributed to the treatment.

Regression

Therapy is most often offered to people who are having issues, people who have moved away from their average ability to cope. Regression, also known as Regression to the Mean, refers to the tendency of groups who are above or below the mean to move closer to the mean on any subsequent testing. This becomes a problem in therapeutic research, as we most often study groups that have scores away from the mean. In a pre-post single group design, where there was a pre-test, and a treatment followed by a post-test,

Preventing Regression from being a problem in research

When a control group is added to the design, then both the treatment and control groups will be exposed to the same regressive tendencies. If there are not pre-existing differences between the control and the treatment groups that cloud the results, then any difference between the treatment and

the reader would not be able to distinguish whether an improvement was due to the natural tendency for group scores to regress toward the mean, or whether the improvement was due to the treatment.

control groups in the post-test can be attributed to the treatment.

Mortality

Mortality refers to the problem of participants failing to finish a study. If the mean depression level at the time of the pre-test was 79 and the participants who were most depressed dropped out of the study, then the mean depression levels during the post-test might be 55, even if there had been no treatment, because those with the highest level of depression scores were no longer contributing to the mean.

Therefore, a single group pre-test, post-test design could not determine the impact of the therapeutic treatment because the result would be clouded.

Preventing Mortality from being a problem in research

When a control group is added to the design, then both the treatment and control groups will be exposed to a similar dropout rate. If there are not pre-existing differences between the control and the treatment groups that cloud the results, then any difference between the treatment and control groups in the post-test can be attributed to the treatment.

If more participants dropout of the treatment group than the control group then there is an interaction between Mortality and Selection (see more on Selection below). When this occurs, results may only be generalized to the demographics of those who finished the study. For example, if younger people dropped out more from the treatment group than the control group, then the treatment effects can only be generalized to those participants who were not younger.

Testing	Preventing Testing from being a problem in research
When there is a pre-test, and that same test is given again after the treatment, it is possible that the persons who took the pre-test learned something while taking that test that might help them do better in the post-test. This research problem is called Testing.	When a control group is added to the design, then both the treatment and control groups will be exposed to the same pre-test. If there are not pre-existing differences between the control and the treatment groups that cloud the results, then any difference between the treatment and control groups in the post-test can be attributed to the treatment.

Static Group Comparison

In addition to the pre-post design, Campbell and Stanley (2015) also warned about another type of non-experimental design, the static group comparison. When two groups are compared and the two groups are not equal at the beginning of the study, then at the end of the study the researcher will not know if the difference between the groups after the treatment is due to the treatment, or if it is just a reflection of the difference the two groups already had.

This problem keeps us from being able to determine the economic value of higher education. How does higher education affect income? We cannot do an experimental study on this, because we cannot take a group of young people and randomly assign them to treatment (you will attend higher education) and control (you will not attend higher education) groups. That would not be ethical. The group that attends higher education is different from the group that chooses not to attend. Generally, it is made up of better students who are more motivated, who come from families with higher incomes, and who do better on intelligence tests. This will not be the case for every person in the group, but it is the case for the group. This higher education group would probably make higher incomes even if they did not attend higher education. The question,

"How does higher education affect income?" cannot be answered to a high level of preciseness because it is not ethically possible to compare equal groups.

Selection	Preventing Selection from being a problem in research
Selection is a problem in research when a researcher attempts to compare two groups that were not either equal at the beginning of the study (random assignment of the sample to treatment and control groups) or when the differences in similar groups cannot be minimized statistically (using ANCOVA, explained later). Because the two groups were different at the beginning of the study, any differences at the end of the study cannot be attributed to the treatment.	When it is possible, the best way to eliminate selection as an issue is to randomly assign the sample to treatment and control groups. If there are sufficient numbers in the sample this ensures that the two groups are almost identical and that they will change in the same way over time. Any difference in the tests scores following the treatment can then be attributed to the treatment. This is gold standard research. Another way to eliminate selection as an issue is to select two similar groups, groups that would normally change equally over time, pre-test them, then use ANCOVA (explained later) to statistically remove pre-treatment differences so the treatment effect will be the only difference in the post-test scores.

What have we learned about research design?

We have learned three things:

1. It is very important to be able to do research that can show that our treatment was able to cause a change. This rightfully is impressive to the reader, as it is more likely that readers will want to use our treatments if they can see that they are effective.

2. It is very important to have two groups, a treatment group that gets the treatment and a control group that does not. Two groups eliminate most of the threats to our being able to show our treatment will help. If it is totally impossible to have two groups, then we can use a time-series design (see page 25) where several observations are collected over time before the treatment, then several more observations are collected over time after the treatment. This design will be discussed further below.

3. It is important that our two groups either are equal (randomly assigned) at the beginning of the study, or that they are similar enough to change at the same speed over time. If they are similar enough to change at the same speed over time, then we can use a pre-test to determine the differences at the beginning of the study, then we can use ANCOVA (explained later) to remove pre-test differences. This would not work to determine how much higher education would affect income, because the two groups (those who attend higher education, and those who do not attend higher education) are different enough to change differently over time.

Quasi-experimental designs

There are several quasi-experimental designs, but we will look at the two that are used most and that would be most appropriate for assessing clinical work. While experimental designs are preferred, quasi-experimental designs also result in causal research. They just must be defended. In this section, a time-series design and a two-group pre-test post-test design will be presented, with an explanation relating to how they need to be defended so they can demonstrate that your treatment is the cause of the improvement in the group or groups you are testing.

Time-series design

A time-series design is a series of observations over time, then there is a treatment, followed by another series of observations over time. It can be represented with O's (observations) and X's (treatments) as in the following way.

OOOOOOXOOOOOO or OOOOOOXOXOXOXOXOXOXO

The first design above has a one-shot treatment, while the second design has a continuing treatment. For example, if we want to determine treatments for weight control the first design would work for a stomach stapling procedure, while the second design would work for a continuing change in diet. They are both classified as time-series designs.

The only threats to a time series design are

- History (this threat can be defended by the researcher indicating that there was no historic event that occurred at the time the treatment started that would have affected the results) and

- Mortality (this will not be a problem if several participants do not drop out, and if they do, results can be generalized to the demographics of those who completed the study).

One of my PHD students, Gitta Trexler, used a time-series design to test her psychological treatment for migraine headaches. Because she had only 23 volunteers (too few to randomly divide into two groups and maintain enough power to find a significant result) she had her participants collect data on their headaches for 12 weeks prior to the beginning of her treatment, and she had them to continue to collect data for twelve weeks after the start of her treatment. The threats of Maturation, Regression, and Testing were removed by the design, because any changes caused by these threats were evened out by the multiple observations. There was no historic event that could explain the participants' improvement, and she had no participants who dropped out of the study, therefore she could claim that her treatment could reduce the severity of migraines, the length of migraines, and the number of migraines (G. Trexler, 1997). She compared the mean of all observations prior to the start of treatment to the mean of all observations following treatment for those three measurements (severity, length, and number of migraines).

To determine if there is a significant difference between the pre-treatment and post-treatment scores on a time series design a paired t-test or an repeated measures ANOVA can be used. These statistics will be described and illustrated in the Statistical Analysis chapter of this book.

Two-group, pre-test, post-test design

The two-group, pre-test, post-test design is an excellent way to do a Causal Study when random assignment to groups is not possible. If the two groups are similar enough to be expected to change in the same way over time, this design enables the researcher to see if the treatment is causing a change.

This is a quasi-experimental design. If one group is much older than the other group, then the groups would likely change differently over time. If one group is a group of professionals and the other group is a group of students, then the two groups would likely change differently over time. But if the two groups are composed of similar participants they can be expected to change similarly over time.

The two-group, pre-test, post-test design can be represented in the following way with O's (observations) and X's (treatments). Each line represents a group.

O X O

O   O

The steps to implement this design are as follows:

1. Select a sample made up of two similar groups, or divide a sample into two groups.

2. Test both groups at the same time on what is being studied (for example, depression).

3. Provide a treatment to one group.

4. Test both groups at the same time on what is being studied. (The statistic for this design is ANCOVA, see Chapter 3. This statistic mathematically removes pre-test differences so any difference in the post-test can be attributed to the treatment.)

An example of using this design would be to study the effectiveness of Resource Therapy on depression. The researcher could start with 40 volunteers who have been diagnosed with depression. All volunteers are given the Beck Depression Inventory II (1996) to determine their level of depression. After 20 volunteers have received treatment for depression, and before the other 20 have started their treatment, a second observation (Beck Depression Inventory II) is given to all participants. If there is a significant difference in the two groups (while controlling for the pre-test differences), using the ANCOVA procedure (see Chapter 3), the study has revealed that Resource Therapy is an effective treatment for depression.

The researcher may then continue with the study and offer the remaining 20 participants treatment to maintain the ethical nature of the research. If desired, further measurements could be made over time to see how well the treatment was able to maintain the positive change.

Experimental designs

Experimental designs are the most highly respected designs, given their ability to show that a treatment was the cause for a change. They randomly assign participants to groups (The sample is randomly assigned to either the treatment group or to the control group. Or, the sample may be assigned to two treatment groups to compare the efficacy of different treatments).

There are several experimental designs, but we will look at the two that are used most and that would be most appropriate for assessing clinical work. They are:

1. The sample is randomly assigned followed by a treatment and an observation.

2. The sample is randomly assigned followed by a pre-test, a treatment, and an observation.

Random assignment to groups without a pre-test

The random assignment to groups without a pre-test research design can be represented (with R= random assignment, X= treatment, and O= observation) in the following way. Each row represents a separate group.

R X O

R   O

The top line is the group that gets the treatment following random assignment, and the bottom line is the control group, the group that does not get the treatment.

The steps in this design are:

1. The sample is first randomly placed in treatment or control groups.

2. The treatment group is treated.

3. Both groups are tested at the same time to see if there is a difference in the two groups. (The statistical procedure would most normally be an independent t-test or an ANOVA. See chapter 3)

Because the groups are randomly assigned, they are thought of as equal at the beginning of the study. Being equal, without a treatment they will change in the same way over time. Therefore, after one group gets the treatment and the other group does not, the only difference in them at the time of testing is the treatment. Any difference in the two groups at the time of testing (observation) can be attributed to the treatment.

A variation of this design is:

R X O

R X O

Here, two treatments are being compared, such as Resource Therapy and Cognitive Behavioral Therapy, without a control group. It is also possible to compare two treatment groups and a control group at the same time (3 groups), or it is also possible to compare multiple treatments, with a separate line for each treatment.

Random assignment to groups with a pre-test

The random assignment to groups with a pre-test research design can be represented (with R= Random Assignment, X= Treatment, and O= Observation) in the following way.

R O X O

R O   O

This design has a pretest while the previous design did not. The addition of the pre-test is more work during a study, but it sensitizes the results even more than the previous design. Both designs are considered gold standard, but the random assignment to groups with a pre-test design allows slight differences in the groups after randomization to be statically removed with the ANCOVA procedure (see Chapter 3).

The steps in this design are:

1. The sample is first randomly placed in treatment or control groups.

2. A pre-test is given to both groups at the same time.

3. The treatment group is treated.

4. Both groups are tested at the same time to see if there is a difference in the two groups.

Just as in the previous design, it is possible to randomize into multiple treatment groups if you want to compare various treatments, such as Resource Therapy and Cognitive Behavior Therapy. Below is an example of comparing 3 treatments and a control group using this design.

R O X O

R O X O

R O X O

R O   O

The statistic for this design would be an ANCOVA. Most studies merely compare a single treatment group to a control group, or two treatment groups.

Chapter 4: Statistical analysis

This chapter provides the information that will be the core presentation of a research article. This information will fit into the results section, and will be elaborated on in the discussion section.

The lights of the whole article will shine on the findings that come from the statistical analysis. Therefore, it is important to get the analysis right.

Even though the statistical analysis and the discussion of the findings are core to the article, the other parts of the article are also vitally important. Because, unless the introduction, the literature review, the methods, and the discussion are well presented, the article will either not be published, or it will not be well comprehended.

It is important to keep a clear eye on the objective. Our objective is to do research and for that research to ultimately lead to better outcomes for therapy clients.

What we need to know about statistical procedures

There are some common assumptions that cross many statistical procedures. *Appendix 6: Assumptions tests* (page165) lists the most common assumptions for statistical procedures and provides a discussion of them.

Gaining a good understanding of the language of research helps us plan, execute and discuss our therapy research. Learning the language makes understanding and communication straightforward. Therefore, make sure you feel comfortable with each of the terms below. That will give you a good preparation for the following procedure sections.

Language

Population

In any study the population is the group the researcher wants to discover something about. A population could be defined as, "Those suffering from clinical depression."

Sample

The sample is the part of the population that data is collected from. If there are treatment and control groups both these groups are part of the sample. Often a sample is studied so we can learn something about the greater population. When we infer findings from a sample to a population, we are doing inferential statistics. If all members of the population are included in the sample it is called a census. For instance, if you are only interested in discovering something about a club and you collect data from every member of that club, then you have census data. When you have census data you do not need to infer findings, because you already have data on the whole population.

N and n

The N is simply the number of people we have in the sample. Little n represents the number of people we have in a subgroup of the sample. For example, a sample (N=50) might have treatment group (n=25) and a control group (n=25). The larger the number in the sample the easier it is to find a significant result. Larger samples are also politically more impressive than smaller samples. Therefore, there should be an effort to get as large a sample as possible, considering cost and logistics.

There should be at minimum 10 people in each group to compute a statistic, i.e., at least 10 in the treatment and 10 in the control group. A sample this size would have very little power. That means there would need to be very large differences between the treatment and control group scores for a significant result. A sample large enough to compare groups of 20 has quite good power. Comparing two groups of 20 allows the researcher a very good chance of finding a significance if the treatment is helpful, especially if pre-testing is completed.

It is not necessary to have identical numbers of participants in the treatment and control groups.

Dependent variable

The dependent variable in a study is the one that is the core thing that is being studied. For example, if you are studying depression, then depression is the dependent variable.

Independent variable

The independent variable in a study is a variable that may have an impact on the dependent variable. If your therapeutic intervention may have an impact on depression (the dependent variable) then the therapeutic intervention is the independent variable. Treatment is a variable, because some participants will have had the treatment and some will have not. A treatment is an independent variable, and what is being treated is the dependent variable.

If you were attempting to predict something like a depression score, the predicted score would be the dependent variable. The predicting variable (e.g., relaxation time), would be the independent variable. The independent variable may have an impact on the dependent variable.

Alpha

Alpha is the criterion that must be met for a significance to be claimed. In social research, alpha is most often set at .05.

Probability of error (p)

While Alpha is a criterion for significance and is set by the researcher, and is almost always .05, the Probability of Error (p) is the result of a calculation, normally from a statistical package. Most computer packages refer to p as sig (for example, sig. = .012). If p is equal to or lower than alpha a significance may be claimed.

Significance

A significant result is achieved when p is equal to or below alpha. When p is .05 or lower, the researcher may make a claim of significance and report the result. When p is over alpha then no claim can be made.

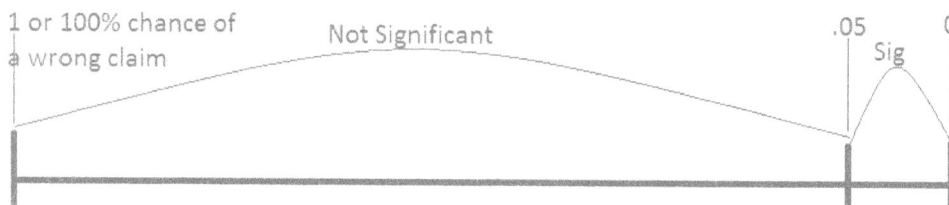

Figure 1: Significance when p is equal to or below .05

Sometimes a researcher will choose not to report a significance because it is not an interesting finding. For example, the correlation between the number of hours worked and income would obviously be significant and that would not be an interesting result. Similarly, it would be obvious that individuals diagnosed with insomnia would sleep less than an average population, so finding a significant difference between these two groups would not be an interesting finding.

Another reason a researcher might choose not to report a significant result is when the effect size is too low to be of interest. If only 1% of the variance in weight is explained by distance walked to work, then that would be of little interest to the reader, even though in a large sample size it could be statistically significant. When comparing large groups (i.e., with large ns) an extremely small difference can be significant.

Metric variables

Metric Variables are variables that you can calculate means on. They can be used in parametric procedures. A parametric procedure is any procedure that calculates means. Metric variables must

1. have equal intervals between each point on a scale (e.g., there is exactly 12 months between each point on the age scale), and must

2. form a normal distribution. That is, they have more average scores with fewer very high scores, and fewer vary low scores.

Most scores from psychological scales, like depression or intelligence, are metric.

Most of the statistical procedures we are looking at in this book require metric dependent variables. If your dependent variable is not metric there are non-parametric procedures that can be run, see, the flowchart to pick a statistic on page 177.

Categorical variables

A categorical variable is a variable where each level of the variable has a name. For example, gender, profession, and socio-economic level are categorical variables. The names of the levels for gender are male and female. Independent variables in many statistical tests are categorical, such as the grouping variable that includes two levels, treatment and control.

Ordinal variables

An ordinal variable is a variable that does not have equal intervals between every level. For example, ranks do not have equal intervals, as there will most likely not be the same intervals between the scores of those who ranked 1st, 2nd, and 3rd. If John was the most depressed, Ava was the second most depressed, and Pat was the third most depressed, they will rank 1, 2, and 3 on the scale.

	Rank	Score
John	1	65
Ava	2	61
Pat	3	49

It is unlikely that the difference between rank 1 and rank 2 will be exactly the same as the difference between rank 2 and rank 3. In the example above, the difference between rank 1 and rank 2 scores is 4, while the distance between rank 2 and rank 3 scores is 12. Therefore, there are not equal intervals between the ranks. If all we have for individuals is their ranks we cannot know their exact placement on the scale, but if we have their actual scores, then we do know their exact placement on the scale.

Socio-economic level is another example of an ordinal variable. There are not exact differences between the incomes of the different socio-economic levels. Conversely, income is a metric variable, as there is exactly a 100 cent difference between each dollar.

Means may not be used in a statistic when an ordinal variable is the dependent variable. Non-parametric statistics must be used with ordinal dependent variables. Because of this, researchers attempt to gather data that is parametric, as metric variables are normally more powerful (better able to result in a significant result).

Reliability

Reliability is a measure of how precisely an instrument measures. It provides no information about what it measures, just that it would achieve the same results each time. A bathroom scale is reliable if you repeatedly step on it and achieve the same result. Getting random results from an instrument would be the opposite of reliability.

Cronbach's alpha is the most common reliability statistic. An instrument that achieves an alpha of .70 or higher is considered reliable. Above .80 indicates very good reliability and above .90 is excellent.

Reliability is a measure of a construct, such as depression, or motivation. You cannot put two constructs, or questions from two constructs into the same reliability analysis.

Reliability of scales (such as a scale used to measure depression) should be reported in the methods sections of an article. You can report this statistic from the literature, and/or you can calculate your own Cronbach Alpha in your sample.

Wang and Gorenstein (2013) report that in 75% of articles that report a Beck Depression Inventory II reliability, the researches check the reliability of the scale on their sample, rather than merely report the reliability from other studies. This is easy to do in a statistical package such as JASP by coding in the respondents' answers to each question. In JASP, a reliability analysis can be selected under the Descriptives tab. This will be illustrated with data further below.

If your sample is too small you will have to rely on the reliability cited in the literature relating to the scale you use. There has been much debate concerning the size of a sample needed to do a reliability test. Yurdugül (2008) referred to authors suggesting sample sizes of 200 to 500 for reliability analyses, but he found using multiple testings that sample sizes for a reliability could be valid with samples as low as 30, depending on the covariance of the items.

Validity

Validity refers to a scale's ability to measure what it purports to measure. It cannot be valid unless it is reliable, i.e., it cannot measure what it purports to measure, if it cannot measure. If a researcher purports a scale measures depression, and it really only measures disappointment, then it is not valid.

Most researches merely report the validity for a scale that already has validity data in the literature. It can be difficult to establish the validity of a scale, especially when there is not another scale that has been accepted to measure the same construct. When this is the case the validity of a new scale may be established by correlating it to the existing scale. To establish validity there must be a second measure of some kind to indicate that the results of the scale match the already accepted measure.

Like reliability, validity refers to only a single construct. A test that has been found valid to measure academic ability, IQ, would not be a valid measure for a different construct, Emotional IQ.

Validity is measured in correlation coefficients. The higher the correlation between the instrument, and the accepted measure that it is being correlated with, the higher the validity. The same coefficients are required for validity as for reliability. An instrument (like a depression scale) that achieves validity of .70 or higher is considered valid. Above .80 indicates very good validity and above .90 is excellent.

Variance explained

If a group takes a test and everyone makes the same score, then there is no variance. No scores vary from the mean. If a group takes a test and different people make different scores on the test, then there is variance. We may be curious about what might explain that variance. It could be that intelligence could explain some of the variance, or the amount of time spent studying may explain some of the variance in the test scores. The per cent of variance in one variable (test score) that is explained by another variable (intelligence) is termed, Variance Explained.

Effect size

Effect Size (r^2, R^2, or eta^2) refers to the actual per cent of variance that one variable explains about another variable. This is a more important statistic than $\underline{p}$ (significance). This is the statistic that tells how meaningful a result is.

The r^2 value is the square of any correlation statistic. It is called the Coefficient of Determination. It refers to the amount of variance either variable in a correlation explains about the other.

The R^2 value also refers to the percentage of variance explained. It is always given when a statistical regression procedure is run, and it is often given when an ANOVA procedure is run.

The eta^2 value is most often the effect size that is given when an ANOVA or ANCOVA procedure is run (explained further below). It also refers to the amount of variance explained. For example, if we are looking at depression, and we are comparing a treatment group to a control group, the eta^2 value will inform the reader about the amount of variance in participants' depression scores that may be changed with the treatment (Levine & Hullett, 2002).

There are other values that are sometimes used to represent effect size, such as Cohen's d. They have values on different scales that must be learned to understand what are lower or higher effect sizes. They can be translated to the amount of variance explained.

The amount of variance explained is a more intuitive and easy way to understand effect size. Cohen's d can only be used when there are only two means being compared against each other. When more than 2 means are being compared an eta^2 must be used. I recommend researchers to just use eta^2 when two means are being compared so the reader can have more consistency in the values being reported, and to give the reader a value that is easier to interpret.

Normally, an effect size of 10 percent is considered low, with an effect size of 50 percent or more variance explained considered high. Whether an effect size is low or high partly depends on what is being studied. If the researcher would not expect any relationship, then a lower effect size might be interesting. Effect sizes below 4 percent are so low they are not worth reporting.

For example, if adult height explained 4% of the variance in people's reading ability that would be unexpected and interesting. But, if intelligence explained 4% of the variance in people's reading ability that would be of little interest.

Significance vs. effect size

We must have a significant result to be able to report a finding. In other words, unless our p value is below .05 then we cannot say we have found something. The sole value of significance in quantitative research is to be able to claim a finding. It is the effect size that reveals how meaningful the finding is. The size of p may have little meaning, but how big the effect size is always informative.

The p value is closely associated with the N, the number of participants in the study. In studies with few participants getting a significant result can be challenging. We would need quite a high effect size to get significance with low numbers, but if we have higher numbers, comparing 30 in a treatment group to 30 in a control group, we will always get significance if we have an effect size worth reporting. Remember an effect size is the amount of variance in our dependent variable that is explained by our independent variable. It refers to how important our result is.

Effect size does not go up or down with sample size, N. Therefore, with a small sample we might get a p of .08, not significant, with an effect size of 30% of the variance explained. If that sample was doubled in size the p might be .02 with the same effect size of 30% variance explained. And if the sample were 4 times as large, the p might be .001 with an effect size of 30% variance explained. From this example, we can see that significance is easy to get with larger samples, while effect size will not change with larger samples.

When someone says that they had a very significant result, that indicates they do not understand what quantitative significance is. People who research large sample sizes will get very low p values with practically everything they run, even if there is less than 1 percent of the variance explained.

Effect size should always be reported, and it should be reported as the per cent of variance explained (r^2, R^2, or eta^2) so the reader can clearly understand the meaning of the results.

Variance, covariance, and residuals

It is important to gain a good understanding of variance, covariance, and residuals to design and analyze therapeutic interventions. Covariance is the same as variance explained.

A good understanding of these concepts clarifies how causal research can be designed when there is no randomized assignment, and it also clarifies how any pre-test can be used to remove pre-test differences so post-test scores can best reveal the power of the therapy treatment.

Variance

Variance merely refers to how much scores vary from the mean. If the mean score in a group is 70 and most people score near 70 then there is not much variance, but if the scores vary from very low scores to very high scores then there is more variance.

Standard deviation (SD)

The standard deviation is a derivative of the variance. It is the square root of the variance.

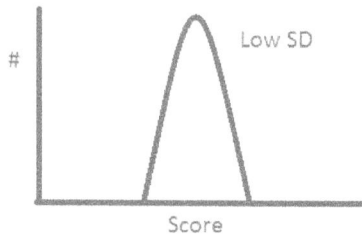

Figure 2: Low Standard Deviation

The distribution shown above has a low standard deviation, while the one below has a higher standard deviation. If two questions on a questionnaire had the same mean and one question had a low standard deviation and the other had a high standard deviation that tells us something about how those questions were answered.

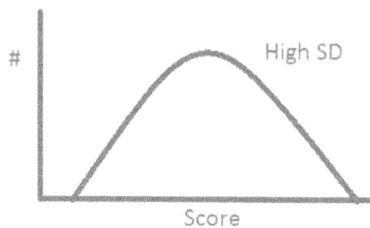

Figure 3: Higher Standard Deviation

The question with the low standard deviation was answered in almost the same way by those who took the questionnaire. The question with the high standard deviation was answered with more disagreement among respondents. Respondents varied greatly in their opinions.

A test with 50 very easy questions and 50 very hard questions would result in a low standard deviation as most people would score close to 50, while a test with a range of questions from easy to hard would result in a higher standard deviation.

When doing research on something like depression, it is better to collect a sample with a lower standard deviation on depression. It would be better to gather participants who were clinically depressed, rather than gather participants from the general population. Participants from a general population would have participants ranging from very low levels of depression, through average levels of depression to high levels of depression. Therefore, the group from the general population would have a higher standard deviation on depression.

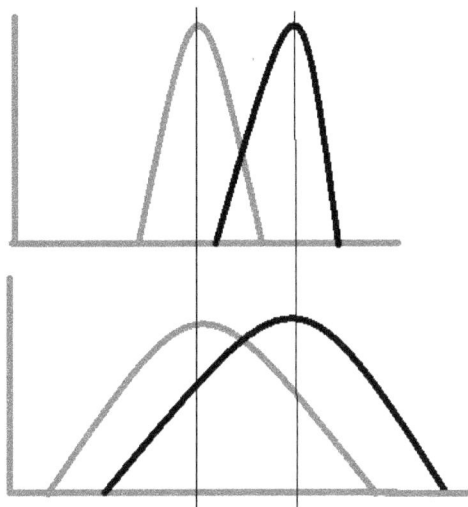

Figure 4: With = means, Low SD's better distinguishes group differences

The figure above illustrates how the exact same mean change in depression levels better distinguishes between groups when the standard deviations are lower. The difference between the groups is the mean difference in the depression scores of the group that had the treatment and the mean depression scores of the group that did not have the treatment.

The distribution represented in grey is the group that had the treatment for depression. Their depression scores are lower. The distribution represented in black is the control group that had no treatment. In the top graphic, almost everyone who had the treatment did better than almost everyone who did not have the treatment, while with the higher SD's in the bottom graphic that cannot be said, even though the mean change was the same.

Understanding this dynamic informs us that it is better to gather homogeneous samples when possible, to have the most power to reveal the value of our interventions.

Scatterplot

A scatterplot is a graphical representation of the relationship between two variables. The values of one variable go along the bottom axis and the values of a second variable go along a vertical axis. Each dot on a scatterplot represents a single person's scores on the two variables.

For example, if John scored 70 on a test, and if he studied 145 minutes for that test, his single dot would align with the score of 70 from the bottom line up and with the value of 145 on the side line across.

When individuals' scores form a series of dots moving from the bottom left to the upper right, as in the figure below, there is a positive correlation between the two variables. Should the scores form a series of dots moving from the upper left to the bottom right then there is a negative relationship.

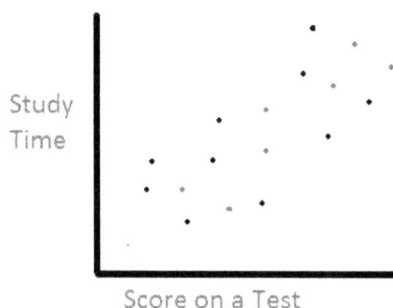

Figure 5: A scatterplot or scatterdot graph

When there is a positive relationship, persons who score high on one variable will tend to score high on the second variable as well, and people who score low on one variable will also tend to score low on the other variable.

When there is a negative relationship, persons who score high on one variable will tend to score low on the second variable, and people who score low on one variable will tend to score high on the other variable. The relationship between absences and grades is an example of negative relationship.

Line of best fit

The line of best fit is a straight line that is positioned to result in the least possible distances between all dots and the line. If we were going to use the value of one variable to predict the value of the other variable our prediction would be on the line of best fit. The closer the dots are to the line, the stronger the correlation, and the more accurate our predictions would be. If there was no correlation, our prediction would be no better than a guess.

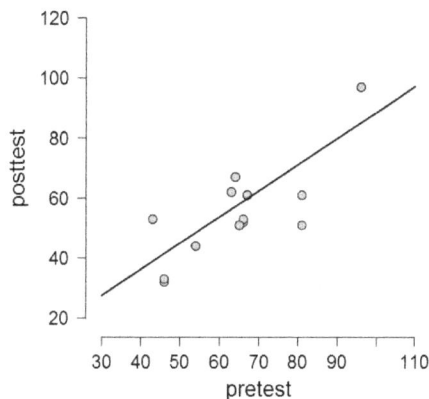

Figure 6: Error is the vertical distance from each dot to the line

Error

Error is the actual variable value minus the predicted variable value.

Consider making a prediction, given the value of one variable below for Pat's score. After the prediction, we discover we were exactly right in our prediction, because Pat's score is perfectly on the line of best fit. We had no error in our prediction, so Pat's error score is 0.

We missed John's score in our prediction, because his actual score is above the line, not on the line. If we predicted John's score would be 9, and it was 12, his score would be 3 above our prediction, therefore John's error score is 3 (12-9=3).

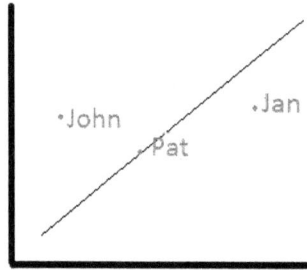

Figure 7: Example of error scores and residuals

We also missed Jan's score. If we predicted Jan's score would be 12.2 and it was 13.5 then we missed her prediction also. Jan's error score is -1.3 (12.2-13.5= -1.3.

In this example with only 3 participants we have the following list of error scores:

John	3.0
Pat	0.0
Jan	-1.3

A list of error scores is called residuals.

Residuals

Residuals is the list of error scores representing the vertical distance of each score from the line of best fit. Each individual will have an error score and the total list of error scores is the residuals.

Residuals are very important in statistics, and they are especially important when doing research on therapy. This section will explain why.

In the figures below, the circles on the right represents all the unexplained variance in a variable, let's say, reading ability. The circles on the left represent a different variable that may or may not correlate with reading ability, i.e., may not explain some of the variance in reading ability. The darker shade represents explained variance (r^2, R^2, or eta^2) and the lighter shade represents unexplained variance. This makes sense, as all the variance is either explained or unexplained.

The first row represents the relationship between adult foot sizes and reading ability. Since there is no correlation between adult foot sizes and reading ability there is no darker shade, none of the variance in reading ability is explained by adult foot sizes. The list of residuals would have very large values.

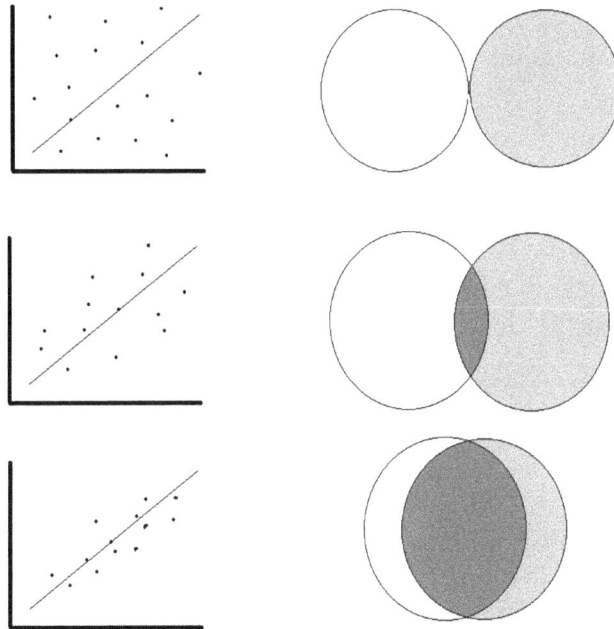

Figure 8: Smaller error scores mean more explained variance

The second row represents the relationship between intelligence and reading ability. It is a positive relationship with the dots moving from lower left to upper right, but it is not a strong relationship so only a relatively small amount of the variance in reading ability is explained by intelligence. The list of residuals would have rather large values. If 15 percent of the variance is explained, then 85 percent of the variance is unexplained. Remember, explained variance is covariance, and unexplained variance is residual variance.

The third row represents the relationship between hours practiced and reading ability. This is a very strong positive relationship with the dots very close to the line of best fit. The list of residuals would have small values.

The list of residuals in each case perfectly represents the amount of unexplained variance. When considering the second row above, the list of residuals represents all the variance in reading ability (lighter shading) that has not been explained by intelligence.

Now is when it gets interesting. Consider the variable on the left below represents pre-test depression scores, and the variable on the right represents post-test depression scores. The pre-test scores were gathered before the treatment and the post-test scores were taken after the intervention.

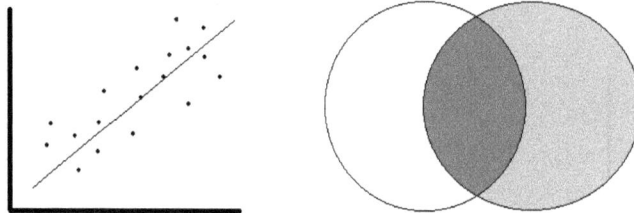

Figure 9: Residuals are unrelated to the other variable

If we were just to compare the post-test means of those who had our treatment with the post-test means of those who did not have our treatment we would get a mean difference, but we would not be sure how much of that difference was due to our treatment, and how much was due to the differences in the two groups before our treatment began.

But, if we remove all the variance in our post-test scores that is explained by the pre-test, i.e., if we remove the darker shaded area, then we would just be looking at differences between the treatment and control that had nothing to do with the pre-test differences. We merely compare our groups residual scores, all variance in the post-test that is unexplained by differences in the pre-test. This way we can tell precisely the impact of our treatment.

We will do this in a statistic called ANCOVA, Analysis of Covariance, and it will be discussed below.

The most useful analyses for therapy research

Because the focus of this book is on causal research, the analyses chosen here are those that can be applied to causal research designs. Correlation is also covered as a useful, exploratory statistic. Further analyses are covered in the appendices of this book for those who want to focus on explaining variance, either as a central part of a non-experimental study, or as an adjunct to one.

T-test

There are two types of t-tests and I do not recommend you use either of them. The reason I recommend against t-tests is because they do not provide either an ability to control for another variable (remove the influence or variance of another variable) and they will not give an eta^2 (sometimes represented as η^2). The eta^2 is the statistic that informs the reader about the meaning of the results.

T-Tests are used to determine if there is a significant difference between two means, usually between treatment and a control means, but also between pre-test and post-test means. It is important to understand t-tests because they are often reported in the literature.

There are two types of t-tests for comparing means, Independent T-Tests, and Paired T-Tests. The paired t-tests are sometimes called dependent t-tests or repeated t-tests.

Independent t-test

An independent t-test compares the means of two separate groups. If two groups have different people in them, such as a treatment group and a control group, an independent t-test could be used. This test will result in a $\underline{p}$ value, but it will not provide the amount of variance explained (the effect size).

An ANOVA procedure can also test the difference between means from different groups, plus it can provide the amount of variance explained (the effect size). The $\underline{p}$ value from a t-test and an ANOVA will be identical.

Paired t-test

A paired t-test can test the difference between two means from the same group. For example, it could be used to test the difference between pre-test scores and post-test scores. This analysis can also be completed using a repeated measures ANOVA, and this latter statistic can provide the amount of variance explained (the effect size). A paired t-test does not provide this value.

It is rather rare to test the difference between pre-test scores and post-test scores in causal research. This comparison may be used when using the quasi-experimental time-series design (see page 25). It may also be used in a non-experimental design where the researcher is content to gather non-causal data. A better use of a pre-test is as a covariate in an ANCOVA procedure, and this will be explained in the ANCOVA section below.

ANOVA

An ANOVA is a statistical procedure that can compare two or more means from separate groups. An ANOVA procedure is only for independent groups, that is groups that have no common members. These are most often the kinds of groups we want to compare when we are doing causal research.

For example, an ANOVA could compare the means of a treatment group to the means of a control group (two mean comparison). An ANOVA can also compare more than two means at the same time. For example, if there were a study where three separate treatments are being compared, Resource Therapy, CBT, and Person Centered Therapy, then an ANOVA could compare all three means to see where any significant differences might be found among them.

A good thing about an ANOVA is that it will provide the effect size statistic, eta^2 (η^2). This is a good reason to use an ANOVA rather than an Independent t-test when comparing a treatment group to a control group.

ANCOVA

An ANCOVA procedure is just like an ANOVA, except it can remove the unwanted variance of another variable. Therefore, an ANCOVA can be used with the two group, pre-test, post-test design to remove the pre-treatment differences, making it possible for the researcher to see precisely the impact of the treatment, even when the treatment and the control groups started out being unequal. This is a wonderful thing. You could the Residual section above (page 46) to gain a better understanding about how this happens.

It is the ANCOVA procedure that allows the two group, pre-test, post-test design to be quasi-experimental. Within the ANCOVA procedure, the pre-test becomes the covariate, the post-test is the dependent variable, and the treatment is the independent variable. The results of the ANCOVA procedure, when set up in this way allows the difference in the post-test to be attributed to the treatment, because pre-test differences are removed statically.

The ANCOVA procedure can also be used to remove other variables from the statistic, such as age or motivation, if desired by the researcher. When a variable is covaried out the residuals that are compared have equal values for that variable for all participants. The test makes it a level playing field for any variable that becomes a covariate.

Repeated measures ANOVA

A repeated measures ANOVA is a statistical procedure that can compare two or more means from the same group. For example, a repeated measures ANOVA could compare the means from a single group, pre-treatment and post-treatment. It could also compare means from a single group pre-treatment, one month after the start of treatment, and again three months after the start of treatment.

Repeated measures ANOVA can also be used to compare any means on identical scales from a single group. For example, three questions on a survey could be compared to see how the respondents feel about three separate cities.

A good thing about repeated measures ANOVA is it can provide variance explained statistics, and it can also control for the influence of other (covariate) variables. Paired t-tests do not provide for either of these.

Correlation (r)

A correlation is a statistic that cannot be used in causal research, as the final statistic. This procedure is to determine if there is a relationship between two variables. It is often interesting to see if two variables are related.

A relationship found in a correlation procedure could be causal or spurious (non-causal). Little kids foot sizes (aged 5 to 10) and reading ability is a good example of a spurious relationship. There is a strong relationship, with kids who have small feet reading at a low level and kids with larger feet reading at a higher level. While the relationship would be strong, kids do not read better because of the size of their feet. Their feet do not cause them to read better. The best way to find out if a relationship is causal or spurious is to conduct either experimental or quasi-experimental research.

Reliability

The reliability of a construct scale indicates whether the items of the scale are getting a precise measure that could be repeated if the same person took the same scale again. Unless a scale, like a depression inventory, is reliable then the results of that scale are random and are unlikely to reveal any significant results, no matter how it is used. When the reliability of a scale is increased, the scale becomes better able to distinguish between groups, as its precision is increased.

Regression

Regression will only be covered in the appendices, as it is not a statistic that results in causal research. It is illustrated it in the appendices because it is a common statistic, and the reader of this book may want to use it in non-causal research.

Regressions are run for two purposes. They can reveal the amount of variance one variable explains about another, R^2, and they can be used to predict the value of one variable, given the value of another variable. For example, we might predict depression levels, given the number of times each week a person leaves his or her abode.

Regression analysis is based on correlations and because there is no comparison of groups, it cannot demonstrate a causal relationship. It is possible to predict a variable with a non-causal correlate. For example, one can predict reading ability in grades 1 to 5, given foot size.

A multiple regression uses several variables to explain how much variance is explained in the dependent variable, and/or to make the best prediction possible. The predictor variables are the independent variables and the predicted variable is the dependent variable.

Running and reporting statistics

We can now look at some statistical packages to run these procedures. We can see exactly how they can be run using JASP, and how they can be reported in a results section of a paper.

Statistical packages

There are several quantitative statistical packages. I will just mention a few and will explain why I have chosen JASP for illustration purposes in this book.

SPSS is an easy to use, menu driven package that will do everything that most therapy researchers would want. If you already have access to SPSS it may be a good choice to analyze your data. It is excellent for data preparation and for selecting subsets to analyze. The problem is that it is quite expensive for someone who will use it only occasionally. Plus, it is not quite as user friendly as JASP, even though it is one of the most user-friendly packages available.

SAS is a commonly used statistical package, arguably not as user friendly as SPSS, and while it is preferred by a lot of people and companies to analyze very large data sets, that kind of ability is not needed for analyzing experimental data. It also would be too expensive for an occasional user.

STATA has grown in popularity in recent years. It is not as user friendly or as expensive as SPSS, but it would be overkill for the occasional user. While it can be driven by menus it is not as straightforward as SPSS, and many users of STATA prefer to write code rather than use the menus.

R is a code driven statistical package. While it is free, there is a real learning curve to learn how to write code to do the various statistical procedures that may be required to analyze therapy treatment data. If you are into math, or computer programing you may want to download a copy of R and have some fun. If you are not a math oriented person, it would not be fun.

JASP is a free statistical package that is menu driven in the same way as SPSS. It has been made to be more user friendly than SPSS, and to use the same type of menu options. JASP is not as powerful as SPSS, especially in relation to selecting subsets of data to analyze. The providers of JASP say that ability will come, but in the current release, 0.8.1.1, JASP is only able to analyze the entire data set that it loads.

For example, should you only want to analyze data from people who are over 21 years of age, you would need to prepare your data set with only those people in it, while in SPSS you could just select age > 21 and run the next procedure. JASP is free, easy, and will do everything we need it to do, therefore it is the package that is being illustrated in this book. If you want a free copy of JASP just download it from https://jasp-stats.org/download/.

Using JASP

 The first step in using JASP to analyze your data is to get your data into JASP. If you should have an SPSS data file JASP will load it directly. If you are starting from scratch and want to create a data file that JASP can load, EXCEL is a good place to start. You can create a data file in any program that can save a txt file, like NOTEPAD, but EXCEL is very easy. Here are the steps:

1. Open EXCEL and type your variable names across the first row.

	A	B	C	D	E
1	id	gender	treatment	pretest	posttest
2	1	1	1	54	44
3	2	1	2	46	32
4	3	1	1	63	62
5	4	1	2	66	52
6	5	1	1	96	97
7	6	2	2	67	61
8	7	2	1	64	67
9	8	2	2	65	51
10	9	2	1	43	53

Figure 10: Excel spreadsheet

2. Type the values for each variable below the name, making sure that each row is a single person. It is a good idea to use the first column as an ID for your participants. For example, ID 1 might be John, and ID 2 might be Pat. All of John's data will go on his row, and on his row only.

3. Make sure to select how you code your data, and keep track of it. For example, you may want to code males as 1 and females as 2, control group as 1 and treatment group as 2. Any score will merely be the person's score on the scale, such as a pre-test score or a post-test score. All data should be coded as numbers.

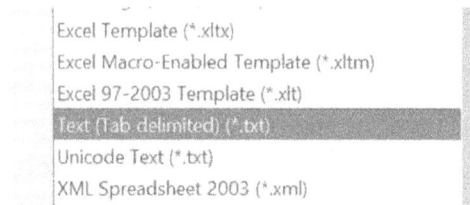

Excel Template (*.xltx)
Excel Macro-Enabled Template (*.xltm)
Excel 97-2003 Template (*.xlt)
Text (Tab delimited) (*.txt)
Unicode Text (*.txt)
XML Spreadsheet 2003 (*.xml)

Figure 11: Saving a text file in EXCEL

4. When you finish entering your data you will need to save it as a txt file, tab delimited. You can do this in EXCEL by selecting SAVE AS and then pressing the arrow down and select the type of syntax you want the file saved as. After saving the file you will be able to use it in JASP. If you edit the file in the future it will default to this type of file when you save it again.

5. Open JASP. At the top select File, then select Computer, and Browse. From here you will be able to find and load the file you just saved in EXCEL.

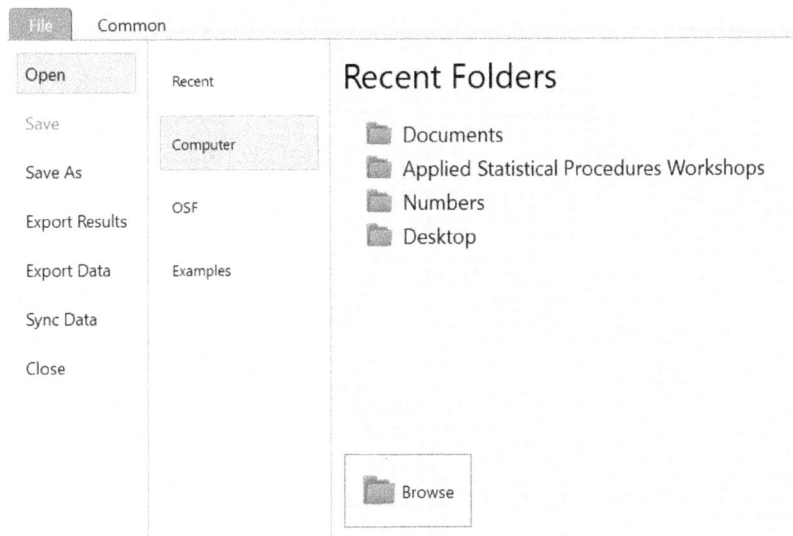

Figure 12: Loading data file into JASP

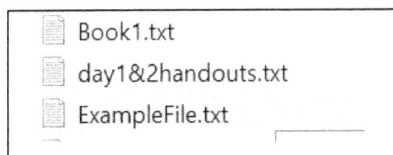

Figure 13: Select the txt file you saved from EXCEL

6. In this illustration, the file was named examplefile. Merely select and open it.

It will look something like the illustration below in JASP.

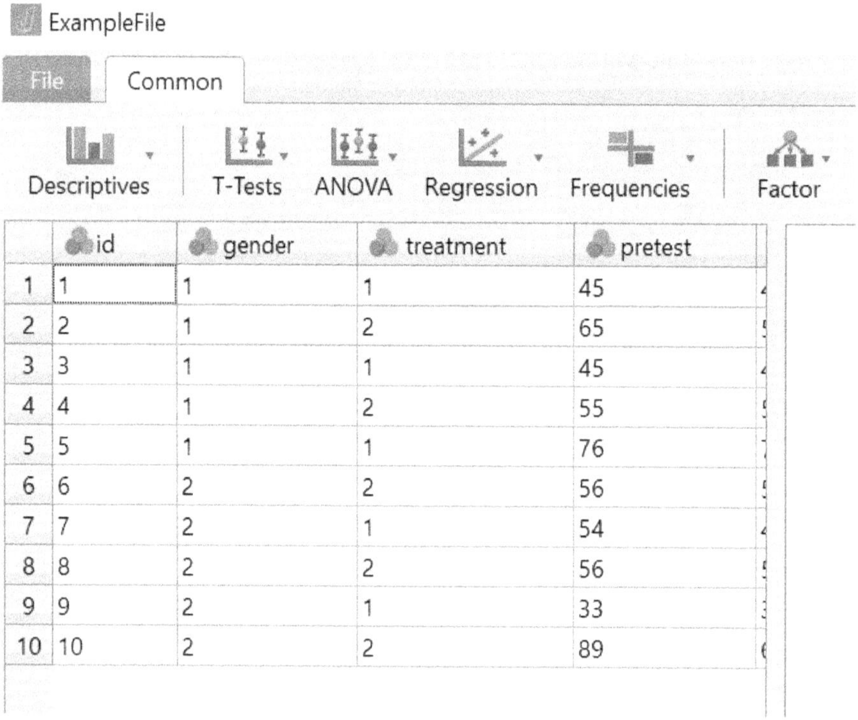

	id	gender	treatment	pretest
1	1	1	1	45
2	2	1	2	65
3	3	1	1	45
4	4	1	2	55
5	5	1	1	76
6	6	2	2	56
7	7	2	1	54
8	8	2	2	56
9	9	2	1	33
10	10	2	2	89

Figure 14: A data file loaded in JASP

That is it. You are ready to start your analysis.

Later, if you want to alter your data set, you will need to return to EXCEL, edit your data, and save it again, and reload the altered data into JASP so you can begin using it. If you save the data file with the same name as before, you can begin using the new data by clicking File/Sync Data/Current/ and then double-click on the file you want to sync.

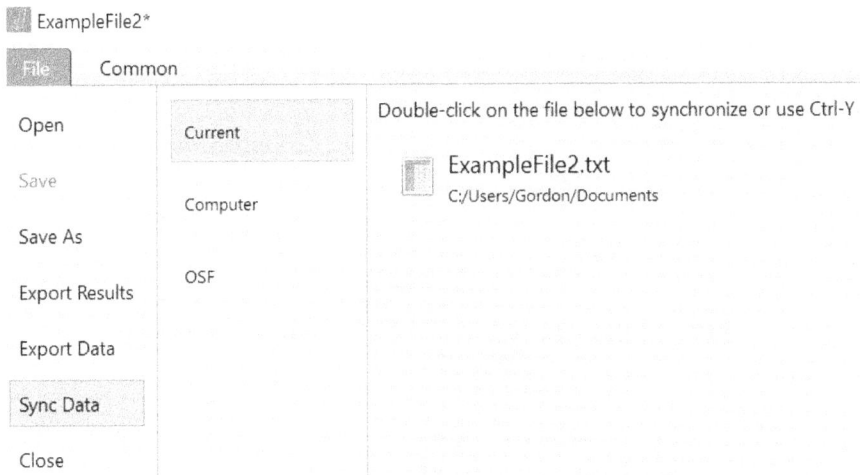

Figure 15: Sync after changing a file in EXCEL

From the sample menu you can also export your results (all statistics you have run) into an HTML file that can be loaded into WORD. You can also copy any single run, or remove it by clicking on the analysis in the output window on the right. Below, I clicked on the word ANCOVA. When you click on the procedure name, you will be given three options.

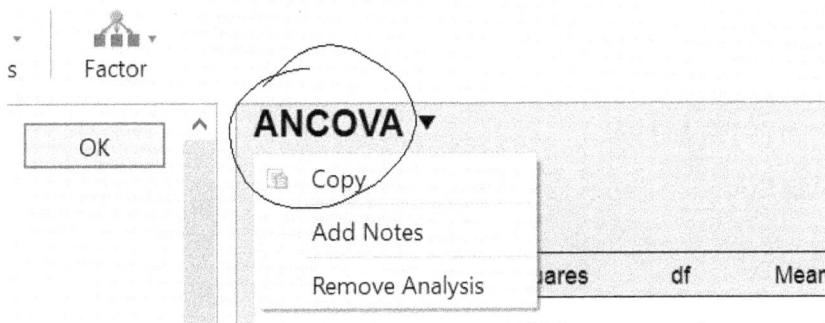

Figure 16: Copying or removing output from procedures

You can copy the procedure output and paste it in WORD (or wherever you prefer), you can add notes to your analysis, or you can remove the analysis from your overall output. You may want to remove some analyses if you do not want to save them when you export your file at the end of your session.

Running and reporting a t-test

Remember, I do not recommend running t-tests, as you can get the same p values from ANOVA, plus you can get eta^2. If you want to work along with the example, the data used here is in the appendix.

How to download a data file from this book and use it in JASP

To download and use any data from the URLs provided in this book, follow these steps.

1. Open the URL by typing it into any internet browser in the address line.

2. In the upper right, click download. You will notice a square open in the lower left with the name of the data text file.

3. Right click on the name in the bottom left and select 'show in folder'. This will show you the folder where you have downloaded the file. You will need this information when you open JASP.

4. Open JASP.

5. Click File in the upper left, then select computer to browse for your file.

6. Locate the file in the folder from step 3 above, and open it.

Independent T-Test

Under the Common Tab Select T-Tests/Independent Samples T-Test

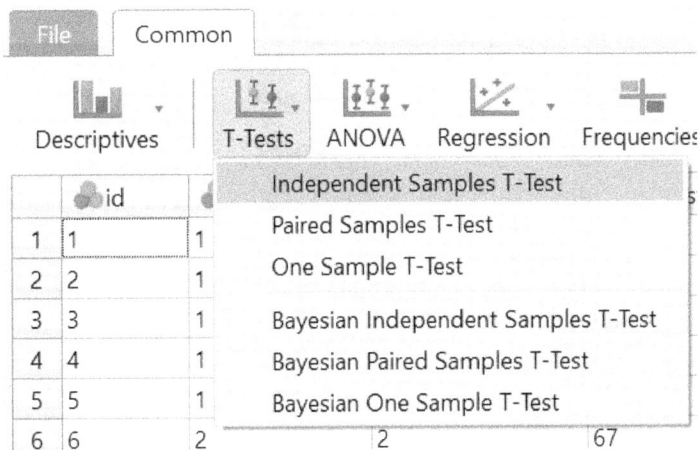

Figure 17: Selecting an Independent T-Test to run

In this example, our dependent variable will be post-test and our independent variable will be treatment. Treatment is coded Control Group=1 and Treatment Group=2. In JASP, as soon as you select what you want to analyze the report shows up at the right (see *Figure 18* below).

Click Descriptives, to get the means of your two groups.

Looking at these results we can see that the mean depression score for the control group is 64.60 and the mean depression score for the treatment group is 50.60. The treatment group had lower depression scores, but we cannot report these results. The p value is 0.056, which is above .05 so we do not have a significant result. Had we had a few more people in our sample the p value would have been below 0.05.

While we could ask for a Cohen's d effect size, I would prefer to run an effect size statistic in ANOVA and get the eta^2 (see page 38), as it is easier for the reader to interpret.

Because there was no significance it is preferred not to report the means, as that could cause the reader to assume there was a difference, when we do not have the right to claim one.

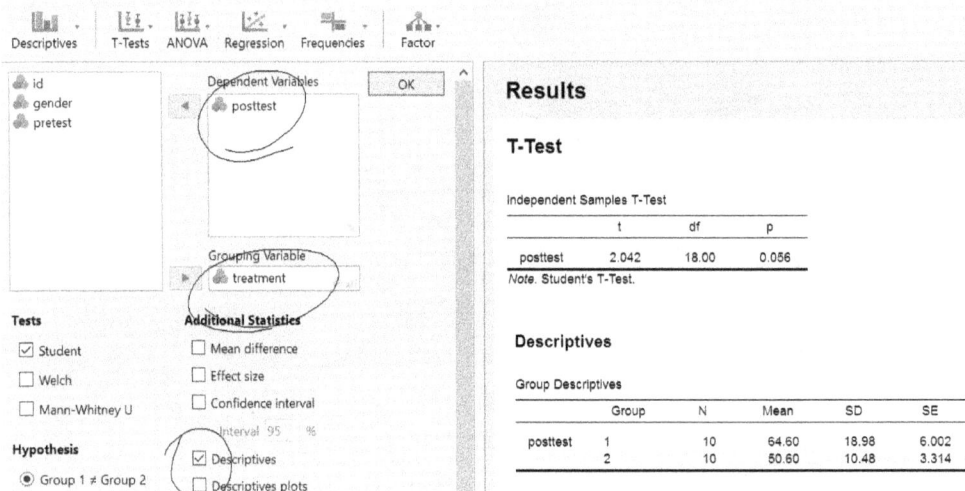

Figure 18: How to run an Independent T-Test

The t value in the table is the dividend when the difference between the means is divided by the 'within subjects differences' (*Figure 4*, page 43, illustrates the relationship between mean differences and the within subjects differences). The higher the t the more chance there is of a significant result. It is the combination of the size of the t and the N that determines the p value.

Results paragraphs have four components, a statement of what was tested, a statement of the statistic used, a statement of the results, and a statement of what those results mean. It is important to use APA syntax (more detail on page 94) when reporting. Below is a results paragraph for this analysis.

We wanted to determine if participants who had Resource Therapy would have significantly lower depression scores than participants who had no therapy. To determine this, we employed an Independent T-Test. We failed to find a significant difference between these two groups, t(18) =2.042, p>.05. Given the small sample size, further research needs to be conducted to determine if Resource Therapy is an effective treatment for depression. The present study was unable to make that determination.

Figure 19: How to report an Independent T-Test

The figure in the brackets is the degrees of freedom from the first table, the t value is also from the first table. The symbol > indicates that p was higher than alpha, 0.05. Had the analysis revealed a significant result the means and standard deviations would have been reported. The sample results paragraph would go into the results section of an article, and further elaboration could be made in the discussion section.

Paired t-tests

Under the Common Tab Select T-Tests/Paired Samples T-Test

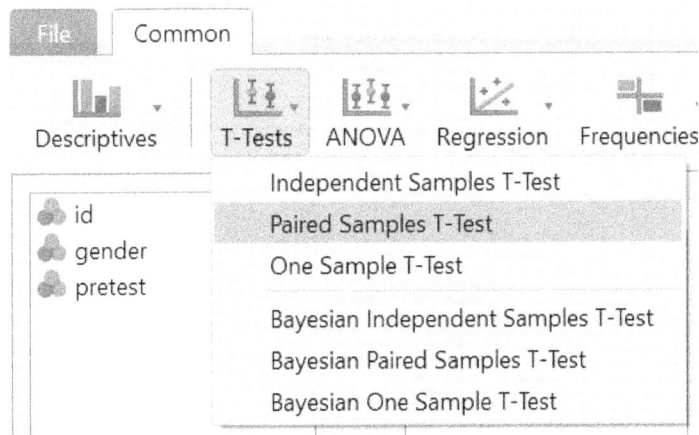

Figure 20: Selecting a Paired Samples T-Test to run

In this example, we will compare the difference between the pre-test and the post-test for the same group of participants. You will need to put the two variables you are comparing into the statistic, and Click Descriptives to get the means (see *Figure 21* below).

This test would be done if all participants received a pre-test, a treatment, and a post-test. Unless this is part of a quasi-experimental time-series design (see page 25) this test would not satisfy causal research methodology, and you would not be able to say that the treatment caused any significant change, see Chapter 1.

A benefit of doing a one-group time-series design over a two-group design is that you can compare larger numbers. If you have a sample of 20, you would be able to compare 20 to 20, while if you had two groups the comparison would be 10 to 10. Comparing bigger numbers increases your chance of finding significance.

A time-series design requires multiple tests prior to treatment and multiple tests following treatment. The pre-treatment mean of all tests can be compared to the post treatment mean of all tests using a paired t-test or using a repeated measures ANOVA.

An additional benefit of a time-series design is that it can demonstrate the long-term effects of the treatment. Following a time-series study it is good to provide a chart showing the scores for each observation from the first to the last. That way the reader can see the long-term effects of the treatment, after the intervention is finished.

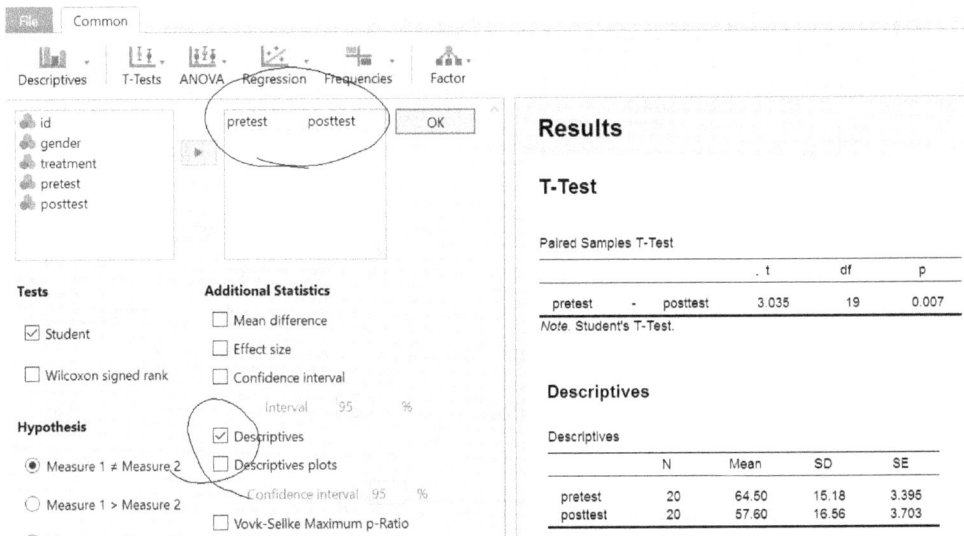

Figure 21: Running a paired samples t-test

Here is an example of a results paragraph for this paired t-test computer run.

We wanted to determine if there was a change from the depression pre-test scores to the depression post-test scores, following a Resource Therapy treatment. To do this we employed a paired samples t-test. A significant reduction in depression was observed following the Resource Therapy intervention, from pre-test (m=64.50, SD=15.18) to post-test (m=57.60, SD=16.56) scores, t(19) =3.04, p<.05. It appears that Resource Therapy is a promising intervention for depression, and that it warrants further research.

Figure 22: How to report a Paired Samples T-Test

Because a single group, pre-test, post-test design does not satisfy the requirements of a Causal Study, the last line in the results statement cannot state that Resource Therapy reduced the depression levels of the participants. It can only state that it is a promising intervention that warrants further study. Had this been a Causal Study the claims could have been much stronger.

Running and reporting an ANOVA

An ANOVA procedure can be used to compare the means of two or more independent groups, so this is the procedure that is recommended to compare all independent groups. Independent groups are groups that have separate members, as is the case for males and females, or those who were in a control group and those who were in a treatment group. This procedure can produce Causal Research results when the sample has been randomly assigned to treatment and control groups, or to multiple treatment groups.

For consistency, I will run the same comparison we ran for the Independent t-test. Under the Common Tab Select ANOVA/ANOVA. If you want to work along with the example, the data used here is in the appendix.

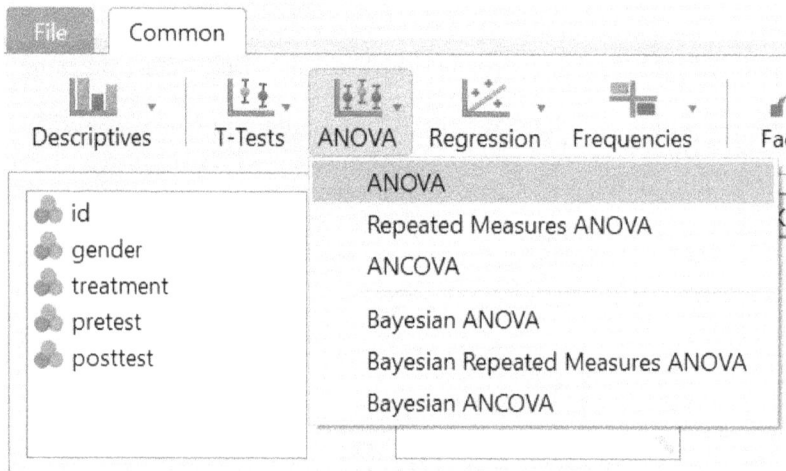

Figure 23: How to select an ANOVA to run

Select the post-test as the dependent variable, and treatment as the Fixed Factor (this is the independent variable). Under Additional Options at the bottom, tick descriptive statistics and estimates of effect size (see *Figure 24* below). This will provide the means and the percent of variance explained, eta^2, which is represented using the Greek letter symbol, η^2.

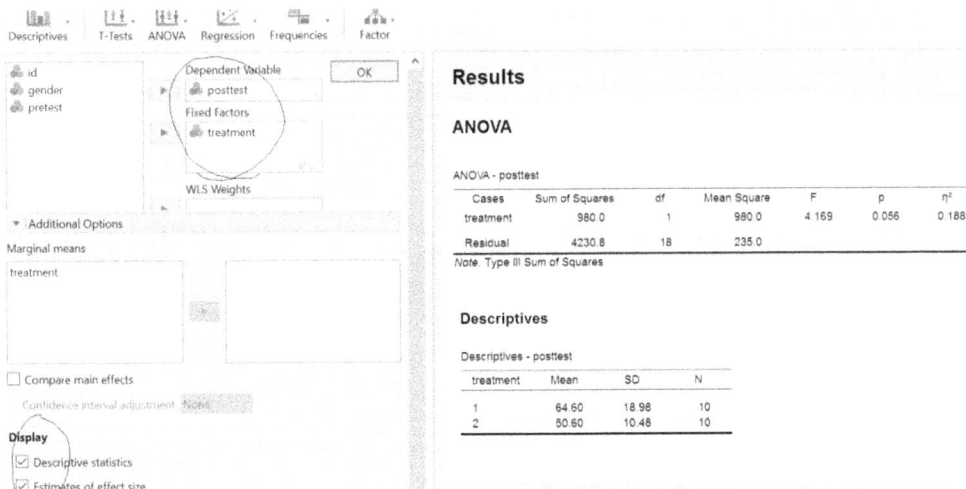

Figure 24: How to run an ANOVA

The F value in the table is the dividend when the difference between the means is divided by the standard error of the mean (*Figure 4*, page 43, illustrates the relationship between mean differences and the within subjects differences, i.e., the standard error of the mean). The higher the F the more chance there is of a significant result. It is the combination of the size of the F and the N that determines the p value.

Looking at the results, we get the same p value as we did when we ran the Independent t-test on this data, but we also get the easily interpretable, η^2. This effect size indicates that the difference in participants' scores between the control group and the treatment group explains 18.8% of the depression variance. While this is an interesting finding we still did not achieve a significant result, so we will not be able to talk about this finding.

The effect size, $\eta^2 = 0.188$ is high enough to provide a good finding and we would have had significance with an effect size that large if we had had a few more participants in our study.

We did not have a causal study, because we did not randomly assign into these groups. But, we did conduct a pre-test so we can get causal results in this study, and we can sensitize our finding with a higher chance of finding significance if we run the preferred test for this design, an ANCOVA. We will do that below, but I will first provide an example results paragraph for the results above.

We wanted to determine if participants who had Resource Therapy would have significantly lower depression scores than participants who had no therapy. To determine this, we employed an ANOVA procedure. We failed to find a significant difference between these two groups, $F(1,18) = 4.17$, $p > .05$. Given the small sample size, further research needs to be conducted with a larger sample to determine if Resource Therapy is an effective treatment for depression, especially since 18.8% of the variance in depression was accounted for with this treatment.

Figure 25: How to report an ANOVA

Because most causal research compares only two groups, I have only included a two-group comparison in this illustration. An example of using an ANOVA with more than two groups is illustrated in the Appendixes (see Appendix 1: An ANOVA with 3 means, page 131).

Running and reporting an ANCOVA

The ANCOVA is the preferred procedure for the pre-test, post-test, two group design. It adds power (the ability to find a result) to the analysis, and appropriately removes pre-test differences in the groups statistically so the impact of the treatment becomes clear. If a significance is found, it enables the researcher to attribute the improvement directly to the treatment.

I will run the same comparison we ran for the ANOVA procedure, but I will add the pre-test as a covariate, thus removing pre-test differences. Under the Common Tab Select ANOVA/ANCOVA. If you want to work along with the example, the data used here is in the appendix.

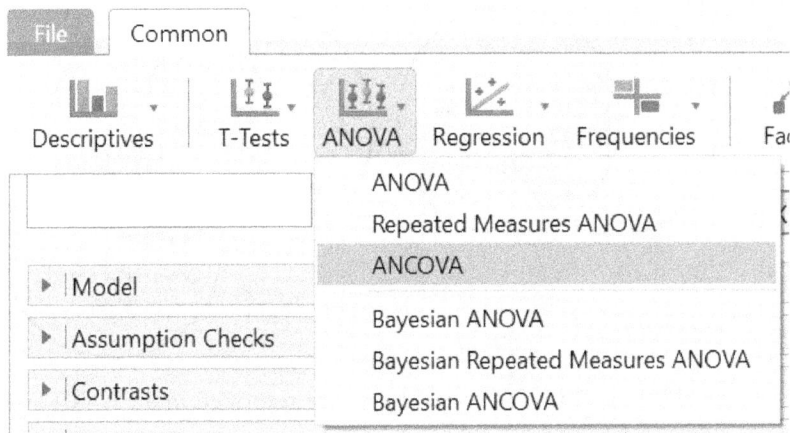

Figure 26: How to select an ANCOVA to run

Select the post-test as the dependent variable, treatment as the Fixed Factor (this is the independent variable), and pretest as the covariate (see *Figure 28* below). Under Additional Options at the bottom, move treatment from the window on the left to the window at the right. This will provide the new, adjusted, or marginal means, that will be a little different because differences in the post-test that were due to pre-test differences have been removed. We will be reporting these marginal means.

Tick descriptive statistics. This will provide the original, unadjusted, means. We don't really need the unadjusted means, but it is interesting to look at them just to see how much they have been adjusted. Also, tick estimates of effect size, then remove the tick on η^2, and tick η^2_p. This will provide the percent of variance explained, partial eta^2.

For ANOVA statistics with a single independent variable η^2 and partial η^2 are identical, but they can be quite different in ANCOVA procedures. Eta squared represents the percent of variance explained in the dependent variable by the independent variable, i.e., the percent of variance in the dependent variable of the darker shaded area in the figure on the left below.

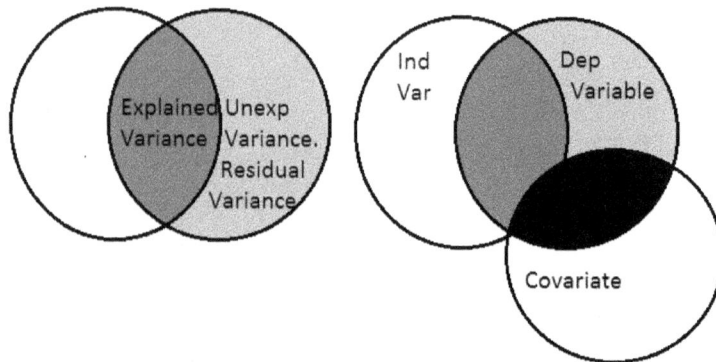

Figure 27: How Pre-Test differences are removed in an ANCOVA

Partial eta squared represents the percent of variance in the dependent variable explained by the independent variable, after the influence (covariance) of the covariate has been removed (see the figure above on the right). When there is a single independent variable, it is appropriate to report partial eta squared when running an ANCOVA. It represents the percent of variance explained by the treatment following the removal of pre-test differences.

ANCOVA - posttest

Cases	Sum of Squares	df	Mean Square	F	p	η_p^2
treatment	1106.9	1	1106.93	24.02	< .001	0.586
pretest	3447.3	1	3447.32	74.80	< .001	0.815
Residual	783.5	17	46.09			

Note. Type III Sum of Squares

Marginal Means

Marginal Means - treatment

treatment	Marginal Mean	SE	Lower CI	Upper CI
1	65.04	2.147	60.51	69.57
2	50.16	2.147	45.63	54.69

Descriptives

Descriptives - posttest

treatment	Mean	SD	N
1	64.60	18.98	10
2	50.60	10.48	10

Figure 28: How to run an ANCOVA

Even though we are comparing the same two groups that we did in the ANOVA above, our results are very different. Our probability of error is now less than 0.001 and we have 58.6% of the variance in depression explained. We clearly have a significant result.

By comparing the adjusted, marginal means to the original means below them we can see that they have not changed very much. So why is our p now less than 0.001 when it was not significant in the ANOVA or the t-test? And, why has our variance explained moved from 18.8% to 58.6%? This can be understood by reviewing the section on standard deviation above (see page 43). The two groups we are comparing were made more homogeneous following the removal of pre-test differences (when we added the pre-test as a covariate).

The F statistic comes from the division of between groups difference (the difference between the means) by within groups difference (the standard error of the mean, or roughly, the differences within our groups). By covarying out pre-test differences we have better homogenized our sample giving us a smaller between groups difference. Because our denominator is smaller, the F is bigger, and that is brilliant for the researcher wanting to reveal the effectiveness of Resource Therapy.

It is possible for the addition of a covariate to raise the p, but that is not normally the case when the covariate is a pre-test. Using a pre-test as a covariate normally adds power to the statistic. A covariate should only be added if it makes theoretical sense to do so. It makes clear theoretical sense to add a pre-test as a covariate so we can better determine the precise impact of a treatment.

Here is a results paragraph example for the computer run above.

We wanted to determine if Resource Therapy is an effective therapy for treating depression. Therefore, in conjunction with a quasi-experimental pre-test, post-test, two-group design, we employed an ANCOVA procedure to analyze post-treatment differences between treatment and control groups, while controlling for any pre-treatment differences by using the pre-test as a covariate. By controlling for pre-treatment differences, differences in the post-test can be attributed to the treatment. Following a Resource Therapy (RT) treatment, the treatment group (adjusted m=50.16, SE=2.14) had significantly lower levels of depression than did the control group (adjusted m=65.04, SE=2.14), $F(1,17) = 24.02$, $p<.001$. The difference in scores between the Resource Therapy group and the control group accounted for 58.6 percent of the variance (η^2_p) in the depression scores. These results reveal that the Resource Therapy treatment for depression, as applied in this research, can profoundly reduce depression levels.

Figure 29: How to report an ANCOVA

These results can be elaborated on in the discussion section of the paper, and any recommendations can be forwarded. The precise nature of the treatment would have been elucidated in the Methods Section.

A further explanation on the utility of using pre-test scores in an ANCOVA

I want to clarify exactly what is happening in an ANCOVA. The covariate in our ANCOVA above was pre-test. Pre-test is a variable that represents the differences in the scores on depression at the time of testing prior to treatment. It is a list of each person's depression scores and all the variance in that variable is 'depression variance'. The whole circle on the left represents these initial differences, the pre-test depression scores. The whole circle on the right represents the post-test depression scores. The post-test scores are made up of the explained variance (dark grey) and the unexplained variance or residuals (light grey).

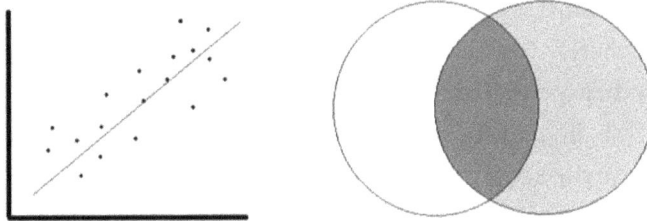

Figure 30: Analyzing residuals

The light grey area on the right represents the scores of every participant after any differences in their depression scores have been removed. This light grey area is called residuals and it is made up of the vertical distance from each and every person's score to the line of best fit. No participant is left out of these residuals.

Notice, there is no overlap with the pre-test scores (the circle on the left), and the residuals (the light grey area on the right). Therefore, there should be no correlation between the pre-test and the residuals. Let's see if that is the case.

A simple regression procedure results in a formula to calculate the predicted post-test score, given the pre-test score. This calculation results in placing everyone's predicted score on the line of best fit, per their pre-test scores.

After running a simple regression, the formula to predict post-test scores, given pre-test scores is (PREDICTED POST-TEST SCORE = pre-test score * .871 + 1.448) (* = multiplied by). This places all predicted scores on the line of best fit.

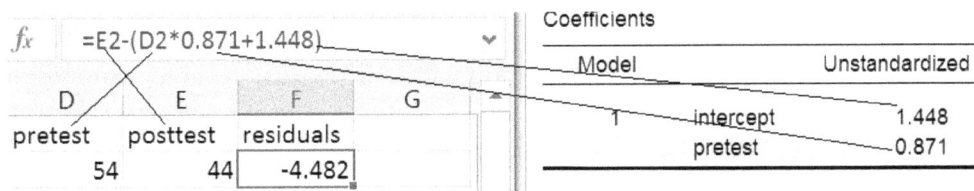

Figure 31: Calculating residuals in EXCEL

You can see where these numbers came from by looking at the figure above, at the right. The regression coefficient for pretest (0.871) is multiplied times pre-test in the regression formula, and the intercept (1.448) is added to the result.

The left part of the figure above is where I created a residuals variable using this formula. I merely took each person's actual post-test score (E2 in EXCEL) and subtracted their predicted score using the regression formula (the score that would be on the line of best fit). Therefore, each person's residual score represents their error score, the amount the predicted score differs from their actual post-test score. This error score is equal to the vertical distance from their actual post-test scores to the line of best fit.

So now we have a variable (residuals) that represents the light grey area in the previous figure. Let's see what the correlation is between the residuals variable and the pre-test. Remember, we anticipated there would be no correlation, because there is no overlap in the pre-test circle and the light grey (residuals) area of the post-test circle.

Pearson Correlations

		pretest	residuals
pretest	Pearson's r	—	−0.001
	p-value	—	0.998

Figure 32: Residual scores do not relate to pretest differences

When we run this correlation we get a tiny correlation of -0.001. This misses a 0 correlation because of rounding errors, that is, the figures we put into the regression formula were rounded to three decimal places, therefore they were not 100% precise. The p-value of 0.998 tells us we would be wrong 99.8% of the time if we said there was a correlation between these two variables.

What does this mean? Since the pre-test variable is completely about pretest differences, and since it has no correlation with our residual variable, that means that there are no pre-test differences in our residual variable. That means our residual variable represents all the differences in depression at the time of the post-test that are explained by factors other than the pretest.

That gives us a precise way to determine the effectiveness of the treatment. If there were no differences in the treatment and control group scores that would mean the treatment was not effective. But if there are differences found in the residual scores in the post-test, then those differences can be attributed directly to the treatment. That is pretty exciting. That is why the combination of this design (two-group, pre-test, post-test design) and this statistic (ANCOVA) can provide results that the researcher can say are causal. We can say, the treatment causes the differences because other differences have been removed statistically.

Because most causal research compares only two groups, I have only included a two-group comparison in this illustration. An example of using an ANCOVA with more than two groups is illustrated in the Appendices (see page 137).

Running and reporting a repeated measures ANOVA

For consistency purposes, I will run the same data for this procedure that was run for the paired t-test procedure above. To run this procedure, we would assume there was a pre-test, a treatment received by all participants, and a post-test. Both the pre-test and the post-test should be metric variables. If you want to work along with the example, the data used here is in the appendix.

The benefit of running that data in the Repeated Measures ANOVA procedure is we can get the percent of variance explained using this procedure, and we could add a covariate, if there were a variable we wanted to control.

Under the Common Tab Select ANOVA/Repeated Measures ANOVA.

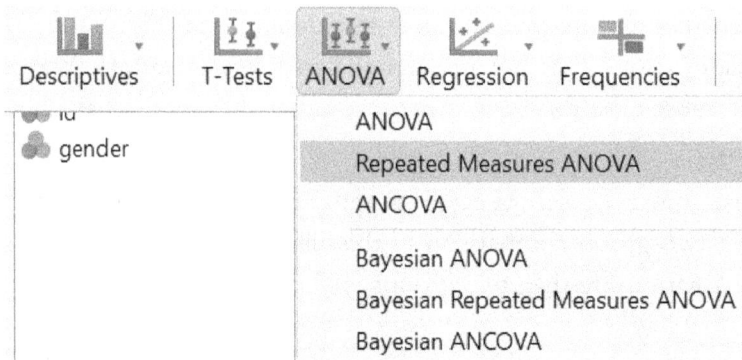

Figure 33: Selecting Repeated Measures ANOVA to run

First, select pre-test, then post-test (see *Figure 34* below), and move them into the repeated measures cells area. When you are comparing only two means you do not have to do anything in the top box, although if you want to you can click on RM Factor 1, and rename it to anything you like, such as depression. The name you give it will appear on the first line in the ANOVA table (see on the right side of the figure).

Next, under Additional Options at the bottom, tick descriptive statistics and estimates of effect size. This will provide the means and the percent of variance explained, eta^2, which is represented using the Greek letter symbol, η^2.

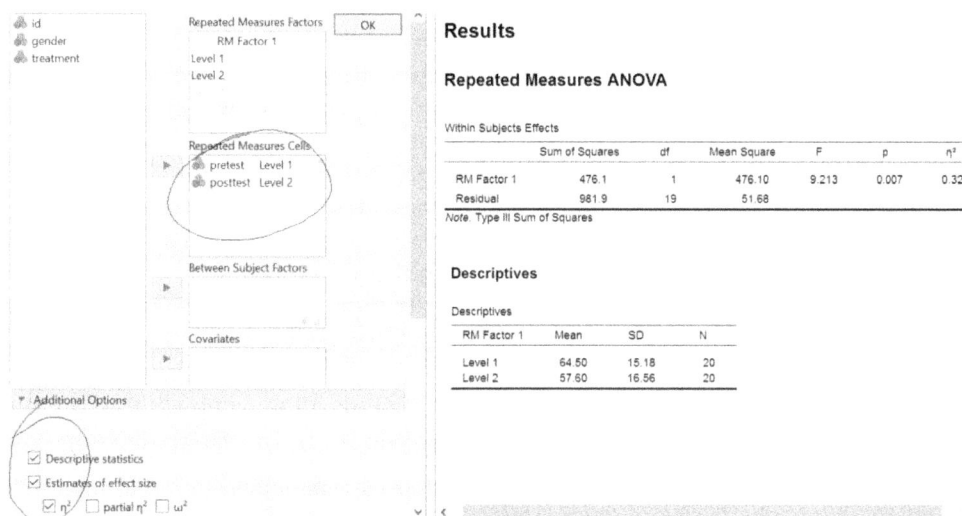

Figure 34: How to run a repeated measures ANOVA

Looking at the results, we can see we have the same p value and means we obtained in the paired t-test. We also can see an η^2 of .327. This indicates that 32.7 percent of the variance from pre-test to post-test is explained by our treatment (The decimal number .327 = 32.7%. A percent is arrived at when a decimal number is multiplied by 100, or with a simply move of the decimal point two digits to the right).

As with the paired t-test, this does not provide us with a causal result, unless it is analyzing results from a time-series design (see page 25). Therefore, we are limited with the comments we can make regarding the change and its relationship to the Research Therapy treatment.

We wanted to determine if there was a change from the depression pre-test scores to the depression post-test scores, following a Resource Therapy treatment. To do this we employed a Repeated Measures ANOVA. A significant reduction in depression was observed following the Resource Therapy intervention, from pre-test (m=64.50, SD=15.18) to post-test (m=57.60, SD=16.56) scores, $F(1,19) = 9.21$, $p < .05$. The η^2 of .327, indicates that 32.7 percent of the variance from pre-test to post-test is explained by the Resource Therapy treatment. It appears that Resource Therapy is a promising intervention for depression, and that it warrants further research.

Figure 35: How to report a repeated measures ANOVA

This results paragraph does not have causal claims that were allowed in the ANCOVA report (i.e., These results reveal that the Resource Therapy treatment for depression profoundly reduced the depression levels in participants). Because this single group, pre-test, post-test design is not a causal design the best we can do is refer to the therapy as 'promising', rather than 'changing'.

Even though this design was not causal, the results still indicate that a change was observed. Other factors may contribute to that change. It is up to the reader to decide if the research gives enough indication to try the therapeutic procedure. It is up to the researcher to not overstate the results of the study.

Because most causal research compares only two groups, I have only included a two-group comparison in this illustration. An example of using a repeated measures ANOVA with more than two groups is illustrated in the Appendices (see page 145).

Running and reporting a correlation

Correlations are easy to run and understand. Pearson Correlations can be run on any metric variables. Under the Common tab, select Regression/Correlation Matrix. If you want to work along with the example, the data used here is in the appendix. This is the same dataset we have been using, so if you have already downloaded it you will not need to do so again.

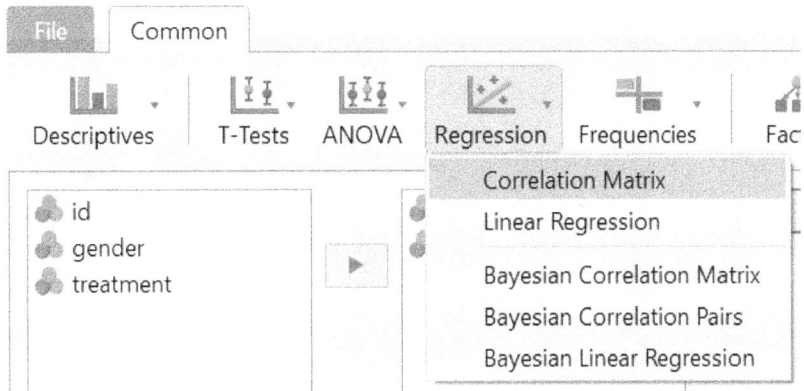

Figure 36: How to select a correlation to run

Next, move the variables you want in the correlation matrix to the window on the right. As you move the variables they will show up in the correlation matrix (see *Figure 37* below).

You may want to click 'Flag significant correlations' and 'Correlation matrix'. You can experiment with those and see if they add value to your report.

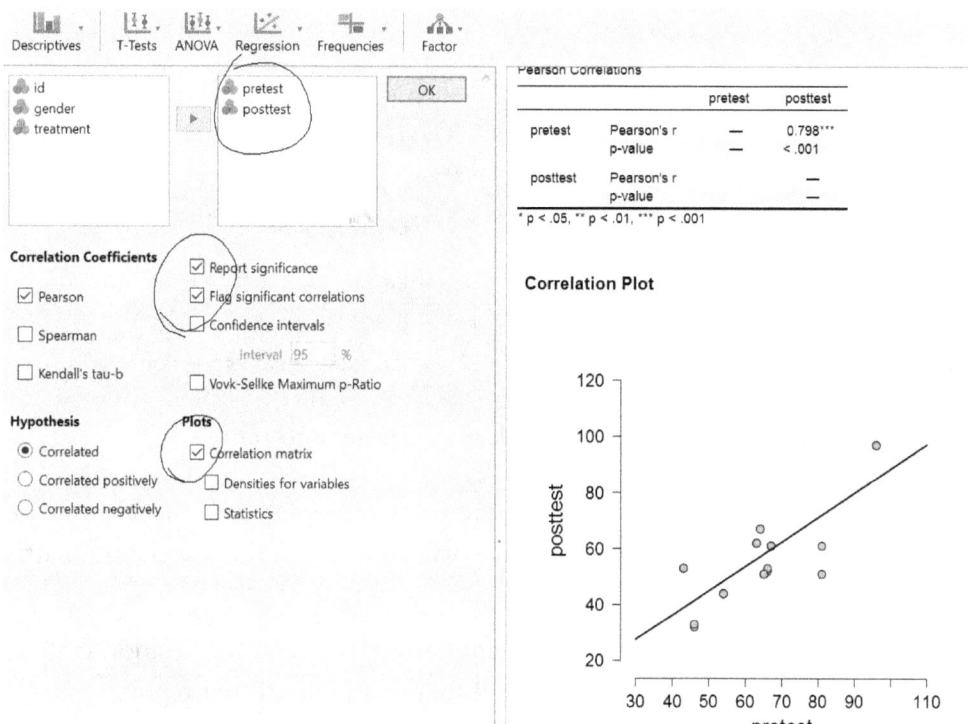

Figure 37: How to run a correlation

By observing the correlation matrix above, we can see a strong positive correlation, as the dots clearly move from lower left to upper right, and they are relatively close to the line of best fit.

We can put more than two variables into a correlaton matrix. The statistic will run each pair of variables in separate correlation procedures, but all correlations will be represented in the matrix. No relationship at all is a 0 correlation, and the further a correlation coefficient is from 0, the stronger the relationship. A perfect relationship would result in a correlation of +1 or -1. These perfect relationships would be exhibited if we were to correlate a variable against itsself. No correlation coefficient can ever be greater than 1 or less than -1. The strength of a correlation has nothing to do with whether it is positive or negative. The correlation that is farthest from 0 is the strongest one.

The Pearson's correlation coefficient in the procedure we ran is 0.798, which is quite high. Squaring any correlation coefficient gives us the amount of variance explained. If we were to square this number we would find we have 64% of the variance explained, and this correlation is significant at the 0.001 level (see *Figure 37* above).

We are not interested in this finding, as we would expect there to be a strong positive correlation from the pre-test to the post-test. It would be very surprising to either find no relationship or a negative relationship. A negative relationship would mean that the participants who had low levels of depression during the pretest had high levels of depression at the post-test, while those who had high levels of depression at the pre-test had low levels of depression at the post-test.

We would expect that most participants' levels of depression would decrease, but participants would tend to maintain their places in relation to the other participants. This is exactly what we found, and that is not an interesting finding. Therefore, this is a statistically significant finding that we would choose not to report. Statistically significant does not mean 'meaningful'. It means you are 95% sure of a result. You could be 95% sure that it is usually daylight at noon, but that is not an interesting finding.

In *Figure 38*, below, I have written a results paragraph for these results to demonstrate the format, but I would not include these results in a paper, for the above reasons.

We wanted to determine if there was a relationship between the pre-test depression scores and the post-test depression scores. To determine this, we employed a Pearson's correlation procedure. There was a significant positive relationship between these two variables, $r(18) = 0.80$, $p < .05$. This indicates that even though participants' depression levels went down following the Resource Therapy treatment (see the repeated measures ANOVA results above), individuals tended to keep their same relative places in the group. It would have been surprising had these two variables been unrelated.

Figure 38: How to report a correlation

The APA style for reporting correlations is to place in brackets the degrees of freedom, which is N-2 for a correlation. The correlation of 0.798 was rounded to two decimal places making it 0.80 and the p was merely reported as less than .05. It would also have been legitimate to report the p as <.001, as it appears in the correlation output. I normally just report the p as less than .05, as p is closely tied to the sample size and large or low p values have little meaning.

The informed reader will know that squaring the r will result in the amount of variance explained, therefore it is not necessary to report variance explained when reporting a correlation procedure.

Running and reporting a reliability analysis

Let's say we have 5 items relating to depression and we want to see if they, together, create a reliable measure. If you want to work along with the example, the data used here is in the appendix.

Respondents were asked to rate themselves from 0 to 100 on how each item matches how they feel, with 0 meaning 'that is not how I feel' and 100 meaning 'that is exactly how I feel'. The statements were:

Item 1: I often do not feel like getting out if bed, even after a long sleep.

Item 2: I can't really remember ever really being happy.

Item 3: There are not any activities I would like to do.

Item 4: I enjoy my food.

Item 5: I would like to travel overseas.

Under the Common tab, select Descriptives/Reliability Analysis.

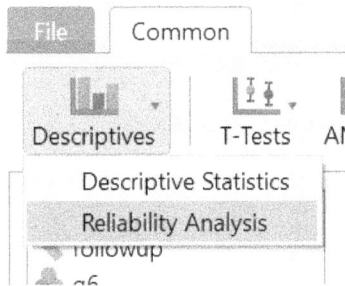

Figure 39: How to select a Reliability Analysis to run

Looking at the 5 items above, we can see how the first three items are phrased in a way that would result in higher scores when the respondent was more depressed. Items 4 and 5 would result in lower scores when the respondent is more depressed. Therefore, Items 4 and 5 must be reversed to get an accurate reliability measure. JASP makes it easy for us to do this.

First, we must select all items that make up our single construct, depression. We move those items to the window on the right, as illustrated (see *Figure 40* below).

Make sure that Cronbach's alpha is ticked and Cronbach's alpha (if item dropped). Sometimes one or more items greatly lower the reliability of a measurement. When this is the case those items should be dropped from the scale to ensure we have a measurement that is precise enough to clearly reveal results, and show any differences between groups.

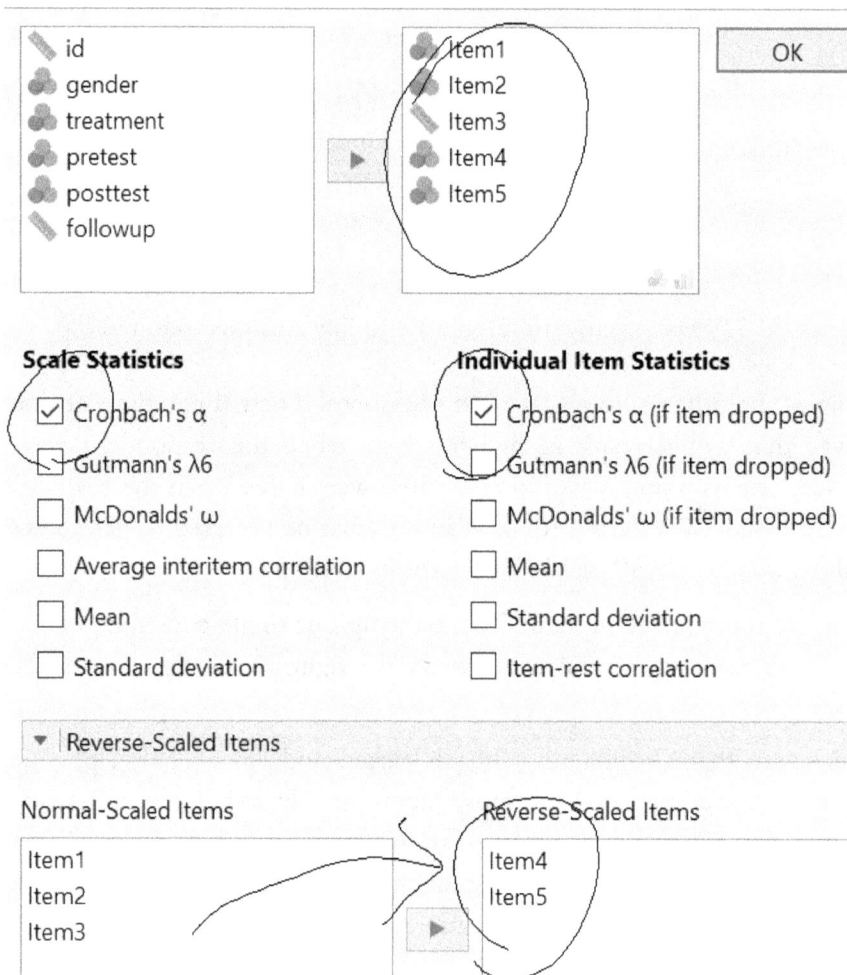

Figure 40: How to run a Cronbach Reliability Analysis

Finally, with this data we had two items that needed to be reverse scored, Item 4 and Item 5. Unless their scores are reversed the reliability would not be accurate.

To reverse the scale simply move the items you want to reverse from the left window to the right window.

Reliability Analysis

Scale Reliability Statistics

	Cronbach's α
scale	0.842

Note. Of the observations, 60 were used, 0 were excluded, and 60 were provided.

Item Statistics

Item Reliability Statistics

	If item dropped
	Cronbach's α
Item1	0.824
Item2	0.710
Item3	0.723
Item4⁻	0.877
Item5⁻	0.854

⁻ reverse-scaled item

Figure 41: Results of a Cronbach alpha reliability

There is only a single score to report from a reliability analysis. In this run that score is 0.842. This is the mean of the correlations of each item to all other items.

We can also look at our results to see if there is one, or more, items that is hurting the overall reliability. In this data, dropping items 4 or 5 would slightly improve the reliability coefficient, but not by much and our coefficient of 0.84 is already very good, so we will not drop any items.

If we had decided to drop an item, dropping item 4 would have improved the reliability to 0.877. We could merely inform the reader that that item was dropped because it was detrimental to the scale in this population, and the higher alpha could be reported. We could report the reliability of .88.

We tested the reliability of our 5-item depression scale (Item 1: I often do not feel like getting out of bed, even after a long sleep, Item 2: I can't really remember ever really being happy, Item 3: There are not any activities I would like to do, Item 4: I enjoy my food, Item 5: I would like to travel overseas). We used a Cronbach alpha analysis after reverse scoring items 4 and 5 to ensure that a higher score related to more depression on all items. The depression scale proved to be reliable with an alpha of 0.84. Alphas higher than 0.70 are considered reliable.

Figure 42: Reporting a Cronbach alpha reliability

We reverse scored items 4 and 5 for this analysis. There is another time when we would want to reverse score these items. If a mean from these items were used as a depression score, items 4 and 5 would need to be reverse scored prior to calculating the mean. In EXEL it is easy to create a new variable that is the reverse score of an item by subtracting the score we want reversed from the maximum possible score plus 1. For example, reversed score= (maximum score on the scale + 1) – the score we want reversed.

Chapter 5: The publishing process

To clarify the process to publish your research I have set out a list of steps.

1. Select your topic.

2. Determine the authors.

3. Select the initial preferred journal.

4. Plan and outline your study.

5. Gain ethical approval.

6. Collect and analyze your data.

7. Write the first draft.

8. Check your references and APA style.

9. Write the abstract and do a final edit.

10. Review the journal's instructions to authors.

11. Submit your article.

12. Revise per reviewers' comments.

1. Select your topic

You may already be clear about what you want to research, but this is a decision that requires a review of the literature. Research is important work and it should add something to the body of knowledge in the field. I once had a research student propose an investigative study for her PhD to discover if there was a relationship between DID and childhood abuse. That relationship had been established in multiple studies following decades of research. She needed to research something that would either add new information, or test the conclusions of previous research.

At the time of this writing, Resource Therapy (RT) is new and is a relatively open area for research. Unlike CBT, which has been extensively researched, RT holds many opportunities for researchers to discover the efficacy of the techniques. RT therapists routinely report rapid changes in their clients. Therefore, it appears that this therapy has a good chance of showing significant results, even in smaller sample sizes.

An essential consideration in choosing what you want to research is to choose something that is interesting and important to you. You will be energized to continue to the next step of your study when you are studying something that you feel is useful. The same holds true when you reach the writing stage. It is fulfilling to write a report about findings you feel are important to offer to the therapeutic community.

2. Determine the authors

Will your article be authored by a single person, or will there be multiple authors? The person whose name goes first is the primary author and that is the person who will decide what goes into the article, and where it will be sent. Any other author has an opportunity to agree or have their name removed from the article. No one's name should be included as an author without his or her consent.

Sometimes it is prudent to add co-authors for something they can bring to the article, such as statistical expertise, access to an ethics committee, or access to participants. It is wise to make sure there is clarity as to whose names will be listed and in what order. After the first name, the order of the other names is not of huge consequence, but clarity can preserve positive sentiment.

3. Select the preferred journal

Deciding where to send your article is not an easy decision. It should be made after considering a few various factors. Some of the questions to consider are:

Do I want the largest readership, or do I want my readership to be local?

If you are offering workshops on the material in your article, a local readership can create local interest in your workshop. Of course, a larger readership will provide more therapists with the benefits of your information.

Will you be viewed as a lay writer, and not considered?

Some journals will only consider publishing articles from professionals in the field who have a specific level of qualification (such as a qualification as a psychologist). It is my thinking that intellectual contribution should not be limited by professional qualification. Both Darwin and Edison were lay authors in their fields, and the world would have been the loser had all journals refused to publish their work. It is easy to understand why a specified level of qualification is necessary to practice (I would not want a lay surgeon operating on me), but the discerning editor, reviewer, or reader, should be able to consider an idea on its merits. Still, some journals will not publish articles from lay authors.

What is the impact factor of the journal?

The better journals have a score called an impact factor. This score is based on the number of times articles from the journal have been referenced (especially in other impact factor journals). Journals with higher impact factors generally have higher readerships. If you are associated with a university, you will also get more acknowledgements if your article is published by a journal with an impact factor.

How quickly do you want your article to be in print?

You may be looking at a lag time of around 2 years if your article is accepted in some journals. If you send your article to a journal that has a good chance of not publishing it, that will extend your time to print, as you will need to wait for your rejection letter before sending it to the next journal. Journals without impact factors are sometimes looking for articles to publish. Lag times in some of these journals may be less than 6 months.

How much change do I want my article to make?

If you do a good 'causal research' study you have a better chance of getting published in a good journal than if you write a theory article, or an article merely describing a technique. If you feel good about the study you have done and if you do a good job writing the article you will probably want a large readership that can change practice. Better journals will provide larger readerships.

Even if you decide to send your article to a journal that does not have an impact factor (most don't), there is a difference in how easily readers can access your paper. Some journals only allow members of the society they represent to ever have free copies, and charge others more than the price of most books. Some journals will not give free copies for the first year other than to members of their society, then anyone can read it after the first 12 months. Some journals provide free downloads immediately after publication. Your decision needs to be balanced between readership, and access to the article.

How will readers be able to find my article?

Make sure to send your article to a journal that will show up on data base searches, such as psych info, otherwise if readers are searching for articles like yours they may never find it. You can see all journals that are referenced in psych info at the following link. It is a good idea to check and make sure the journal you send your article to is on this list, otherwise pick a different journal.

http://www.apa.org/pubs/databases/psycinfo/coverage.aspx.

4. Plan and outline your study

One of the most helpful steps is to plan your study and outline the article you will write. Not much gets done when you are not clear on what you are supposed to do. Make clear plans. Decide on the research design (see the design section of this book), plan the numbers of participants, how the participants will be accessed, and the instruments that will be used.

Put all headings in your article, including the heading for the abstract, even though that will be the last thing you will write. You can always change things as you go along, but it is good to have a plan.

When you have structured your article, then all you need to do is fill in the gaps. You will then know what you need to do. It is very helpful to know you have a plan and to know exactly where you are in that plan at any given time.

It is prudent to begin writing your article even before you collect your data. Write your introduction and literature review so you will have a better idea about the scope of what you are doing, and so you will know exactly what you need to do. Writing these before you finish your planning will motivate you and will instruct you.

It is very helpful to write your methodology section before you finish collecting data. It is a great feeling to be able to write the results section and the discussion section immediately following the data collection. Everything is fresh and you are ready to write. Why not make it easier on yourself and most fun for yourself and write the first three sections so when you get your data, all you need to write is the results and the discussion? You will be doing an overall edit at the end.

5. Gain ethical approval

Detailing ethical requirements for research on human subjects is not the focus of this book. Researchers must attend to factors such as informed consent, confidentiality, truly voluntary participation, rights of participants, and the local requirements to gain ethical approval by an appropriate committee. These requirements vary according to the precise type of research being conducted, the country where the research is conducted, and the journal where the article is submitted.

Ethical approval is required for research on human subjects in most OECD countries. If you, or a co-author, are associated with an institution, such as a university or a hospital, it is likely that your institution will have its own approved ethics committee. If not, and if you are doing human research, you will need to find an approved committee to review your research. Most journals will want a statement of review with a verification ethical review number.

When planning your research, be aware that ethical approval can be time-consuming, and in some countries, there is an expense involved. Many ethics committees will consider ethics proposals from individuals who are not directly associated with their institution, although there may be a fee involved.

It is sometimes prudent to co-author with a person who has an association with an institution that has an approved ethics committee. If you are planning research on Resource Therapy you can contact ResourceTherapyInternational.com for assistance in finding a co-author near you who has access to an approved ethics committee.

6. Collect and analyse your data

How good are you at following instructions? When you planned and outlined your study, you wrote the instructions you need to follow to collect and analyze your data. All you need to do now is be your own best employee. Do what you said you were going to do.

The actual data collection process is not the hardest part of research. It is usually rather straightforward. And, the analysis of your data will also be straightforward if you follow your design plan and use the statistical selection flowchart provided in this book (Appendix 8: Flowchart to pick a statistic, page 177).

It is fun to get data in, and to analyze it. You, of course, will hope for significance. If you fail to get significance your chance of a publication is much reduced, plus you want to be able to show how your therapy works. If you have a good technique, and if you have a decent sample size (20 in each compared group) you should get significance. Just follow the appropriate sections in this book to analyze and report your findings.

7. Write the first draft

If you write the introduction, the literature review, and the methodology before data collection is finished, finishing your draft will be easier. Don't worry if you have not finished these sections. Most researchers have not. But, if you did write those sections before the completion of data collection, the first draft is already in sight.

When finishing the first draft make sure the pieces fit together making a nice story flow. The reader needs to be captured by your article.

The first draft means everything is there. It does not mean it is ready to send off. Still, it is a very good feeling to finish the first draft. You have conceived, planned, executed, analyzed and written your research. That's impressive.

It is not the mission of the first draft to be perfect. Its mission is to be inclusive of all that needs to be there.

8. Check your APA style and references

Make sure you know where you will be sending your article. While it is almost certain that the journal you choose to send your therapy article to will require an APA formatting style, journals vary in their formatting requirements. They vary both in the length and in the structure of the articles they will consider.

Importance of formatting

Editors are very busy. They spend a lot of time working with the articles that are sent to their journals and when they see an article come in that needs a lot of formatting work, they are likely to decline from spending all the time to communicate back and forth with the author to get the article ready to publish.

But, if they get an article that is near perfect in format and style, they see something that would take minimal work preparing to publish. You are much more likely to get a publication if you spend the time to find out exactly the format expected by the journal editors where you are sending your article, and follow their expectations.

Most journals have a section or a website that details the expectations of the editors. It is also a good idea to look at a few editions of the journal where you are sending your article and match your article to the style of the ones that have been successfully published.

APA style

Most journals that publish therapy related articles employ APA (American Psychological Association) style. This refers to the style of referencing in text and in the reference list. It also refers to how to appropriately report statistical results in the results section.

APA also makes suggestions as to what should be included in the different parts of an article, such as in the Methods, and in the Results sections. Occasionally, a journal will have requirements that vary from the APA guidelines, or that extend beyond them.

You are only allowed to send an article to a single journal for review at a time. You may send it to another journal only after the first journal has rejected it, or after you have withdrawn it from consideration. (You can send a book to multiple publishers at the same time for consideration.)

The illustrations in this text employ APA style throughout, and it is easy to find APA style syntax online with a simple search. Put in what you want help with and APA style (i.e., 'citing a paper with 2 authors' and APA style).

References

Make sure all articles in your reference list have been cited in text, and make sure all citations are listed in the reference list.

Some journals ask for you to include DOIs in the reference list, when they are available. A DOI is a digital object identifier that is used to make finding articles easier. If an article in your reference list has a DOI you can find it by going to http://search.crossref.org/ and entering the exact title of the article. For example, at that site, if you enter 'Sensory Experience Memory in Resource Therapy' it will return the digital object identifier, https://doi.org/10.1080/00207144.2017.1246882. This is a link address that goes to information about the article, including an abstract and how to obtain a full copy. The DOI will go at the end of the citation in the references.

For example:

Emmerson, G. J., (2017). Sensory experience memory in Resource Therapy. International Journal of Clinical and Experimental Hypnosis, 65(1), 120-131. Doi: 10.1080/00207144.2017.1246882

9. Write the abstract and do a final edit

Following the completion of writing your article, you will be ready to write a summary of it. Some journals want an abstract in heading format, but most just want a paragraph. Follow the journal's requirements for length and format.

You should make sure your abstract is well written, as it is what will convince readers if yours is an article worth reading. The entire study should be summarized, including the core results.

You should make some effort to incorporate any key search terms into your abstract, more than once if you can do so, while keeping an easy flow. Search terms in the abstract will help readers find your article when they are searching data bases.

Below is a list of issues editors have flagged as problems with submitted articles (Bartol, 1983, cited in Eichorn & VandenBos, 1985). It is a good idea to look at this list before submitting your article to make sure you have already attended to these.

- inadequate review of the literature

- inappropriate citations

- unclear introduction

- ambiguous research questions

- inadequately described sample

- insufficient methodology

- incompletely described measures

- unclear statistical analysis

- inappropriate statistical techniques

- poor conceptualization of discussion

- discussion that goes beyond the data

- poor writing style

- excessive length

10. Review the journal's instructions to authors

There are times when it pays to follow instructions. Preparing an article for publication is one of those times.

11. Submit your article

You know it is good. Press the button and enjoy yourself while it is being reviewed. You may be able to have quite a good time, as the review process may take a while. The approximate length of time the review process will take should be made clear in the journal's information to contributors.

12. Revise per reviewers' comments

Be prepared for whatever reply you receive from the editor. When you hear back from a journal it will either be accepted as is (very rare), accepted with changes (winner), or rejected (crazy reviewers).

It is rare for an article to be accepted without changes being requested. Some reviewers can be scathing in their remarks. Be prepared for this. If you do not get an outright rejection, you are a winner. If you do get a rejection, you have merely sent it to one journal. You can make any changes you would like (or not) and send it to a second journal.

Requests for changes can, at first, look daunting, but all you need to do is type out each request and indicate how you have attended to it. You have the benefit of having a list of things that need to be done, and you merely diplomatically attend to each one. Show appreciation to the editor and the reviewers for taking their time to help make it a better article, even if you may not feel the positive feelings you report.

When you return your article, make it crystal clear how you have attended to each change. Your list of changes should include the page and paragraph number where each change can be noted in the article. Editors who feel appreciated and attended to, are more eager to get your article in print. Your mission is to bring your findings to the readers of the journal, and to get your findings into data bases where others can benefit from your information.

The next chapter provides a detailed illustration for writing a research article.

Chapter 6: Writing your article

This chapter will illustrate how to apply what we have learned. The results illustrated in the section on ANCOVA (page 68) will be used as an example for structuring and writing a research article in APA style.

The first section of this chapter will give a brief overview of Resource Therapy (Emmerson, 2014a) to place it into context for the article illustrated below. The proceeding sections will illustrate a written research article.

The reader needs to keep in mind that this article is produced only for illustration purposes. Like all analyses in this book the data was created expressly for illustration purposes and it does not come from an actual research project. That explains why the depression scores presented here do not correspond with the actual ranges of the scale.

All referencing for this illustrated article is APA style, and the studies referenced are real, to exemplify how research of this type is supported with literature. The statements regarding the nature and techniques of Resource Therapy are also accurate.

Resource Therapy

Resource Therapy (RT) is a psychotherapy based on the concept that the personality is composed of separate parts, Resource States. When these personality parts are normal and healthy, they are the resources that help us achieve, play, socialize, and rest. When they are pathological, they interfere with our ability to internalize and react in the manner we would prefer.

A client will present to a therapist most often in a normal, healthy resource state that complains about another state that either acts in an unwanted way (i.e., gambles, overeats, abuses) or experiences unwanted emotions (i.e., fear, unworthiness, anxiety). If the therapist continues to engage with the healthy, reporting state, the chance of achieving rapid and lasting change is limited.

Resource therapists move directly to the pathological resource state that needs change, rather than continuing to engage with the reporting state. An analogy to this would be a student in a classroom reporting that another student is upset. It would be of little benefit to the upset student if the teacher just continued talking with the reporting student, rather than talk directly with the upset student.

Resource therapists see pathological states as being either

- Retro (conducting unwanted behavior),

- Vaded (experiencing unwanted emotions),

- Conflicted (states fighting over which will use the time, as in a state that wants work to be done and a state that wants to rest or play), or

- Dissonant (when a state is holding the conscious and it does not want to; when a different state would be a better state to hold the conscious).

Resource Therapy has RT Actions (specified techniques) that are specific for the type of pathology a state experiences.

While the article illustrated below was based on data created for illustration only, it would be a good study for a Resource Therapist to conduct.

The Resource Therapy treatment for depression is to locate and engage with two resource states that have enjoyed activities in the past that could be enjoyed today, if the client were not depressed. The RT therapist brings into the conscious each of these states and gains a commitment that they will again engage in the positive activity that they enjoyed in the past, if given permission to do this by the state that is depressed.

Depression is viewed in RT theory as a disappointed state refusing to give permission to other resource states to engage in life and enjoy living. Therefore, it is important to find states that are willing to engage positively, and to get permission for these states to do so.

Following speaking with two states that have committed to engage positively, the RT therapist engages directly with the depressed state, shows compassion and understanding for this state, and asks this state for permission for the two positive states to begin engaging again. The depressed state, if it feels appreciated and understood, will grant this permission and the client can begin the process of rebuilding positive energy.

This is similar to a cognitive behavioral technique of asking the client to begin re-engaging, but by getting permission from the depressed state, and by having that state to speak directly to the positive states in giving that permission, the client finds it much easier to begin re-engaging.

Further work with the client is with the depressed state to find a way it can use its skills to contribute in the future. When this state again sees a positive role for itself, it will stop blocking other resource states from enjoying positive activities.

Below, is an example of a research article with a quasi-experimental design. Each section of the article includes explanatory information presented inside a shaded box. Information in these boxes do not form part of the article.

All research articles can have the same sections illustrated below. You merely describe your particular design in the methodology section.

Title: The efficacy of a four-week Resource Therapy intervention on clinical depression

Abstract

"The title and the abstract are key elements that inform the reader of the contents of the manuscript and, as a rule, are the parts of the manuscript that gain the widest exposure" (American Psychological Association, 2010, p. 7).

(See pages 13 and 95 to review more information on abstracts). Note: Resource Therapy and depression are key words listed 5 and 4 times respectively (see page 13).

Resource Therapy (RT) is a new psychotherapy based on neuroscientific evidence that the personality is composed of parts. It has been expanding rapidly in popularity with training now offered around the world. While its rapid expansion appears due to therapists appreciating what they perceive are powerful interventions, there has been little scientific investigation into its efficacy. This study utilized a quasi-experimental pre-test, post-test, two group design to determine if those who had a 4-week treatment in Resource Therapy, had significantly lower depression levels than a control group. The slight pre-test differences between the groups were statistically controlled in an Analysis of Covariance procedure, to sensitize the research and better evaluate the Resource Therapy treatment. Participants who had the 4-week treatment had significantly lower levels of depression than those in the control group. While more study is needed on Resource Therapy, this study indicates that Resource Therapy resulted in positive results for participants who suffered from depression. The treatment described and utilized in this study accounted for 58.6% of the variance in depression scores.

Introduction and literature review

Most articles meld the introduction and the literature review into one section.

"A strong introduction engages the reader in the problem of interest and provides a context for the study at hand. In introducing the research concern, the writer should provide a clear rationale for why the problem deserves new research, placing the study in the context of current knowledge and prior theoretical and empirical work on the topic." (American Psychological Association, 2010, p. 7)

(See pages 14 and 90 to review more information on writing these sections)

Psychological Depression can be devastating to individuals and families, and it costs the economy both in lost work hours and in treatment costs. The current most preferred treatment methods are aimed at merely managing depression, along with the need for ongoing medication, rather than bringing a cessation to the symptoms. A disturbing number of individuals have resigned to taking anti-depressant medication for many years. Resource Therapy is a relatively new, short-term treatment for depression, and for other psychological disturbances. Anecdotal evidence suggests that a Resource Therapy treatment can rapidly reduce depressive symptoms without the need for medication.

Depression is not a new disturbance. It was reported by the Egyptians over two-thousand years ago, and it likely presented well before those reports. A Greek physician, Hippocrates (460-370 BC), believed 'melancholy' was cause by an imbalance in bodily fluids (Kielkiewicz & Kennedy, 2015). As early as the 1700's, melancholy was associated with diet, sleep, music, work, and companionship (Burton, 1932). French psychiatrist, Louis Delasiauve, referred to melancholy as 'depression' in 1856, and by the 1860s the referencing to 'depression' was so widespread it had been placed in medical dictionaries (Berrios, 1988).

From those early days to the present, there have been literally thousands of articles on depression. It has been dissected, re-divided, and evaluated. Some types of depression include

- Atypical Depression (AD),

- Melancholic Depression,

- Psychotic Major Depression (PMD),

- Catatonic Depression,

- Postpartum Depression (PPD),

- Seasonal Affective Disorder (SAD),

- Dysthymia,

- Double Depression,

- Depressive Disorder Not Otherwise Specified (DD-NOS),

- Depressive Personality Disorder (DPD),

- Recurrent Brief Depression (RBD), and

- Minor Depressive Disorder (American Psychiatric Association, 2013).

Manic depression (a bipolar disorder) is a different disorder.

The present study is about melancholic depression, characterized by feelings of sadness, low energy and inability to engage positively in living. For simplicity in expression, this is what will be referred to in this article as, 'depression'.

Even though depression sits on a mountain of research, there is little agreement among different psychological professions, and professionals form different therapeutic orientations as to what causes it. "In psychiatry, depression is perceived as a neurological reaction to an imbalanced level of hormones or other neurochemicals (Kielkiewicz & Kennedy, 2015, p. 5). Because psychiatrists see depression as a chemical imbalance, they attempt to use pharmaceuticals to restore a chemical balance. One problem with this is the chronic nature of the treatment. Antidepressants are often taken for many years to relieve a perceived chemical imbalance.

Psychoanalysts view depression symptoms as resulting from repressed feelings. They view psychoanalytic therapy as the best way to relieve depression (Kielkiewicz & Kennedy, 2015, p. 5).

Cognitive behaviorists hold that those who suffer from depression need to reframe their thinking, and re-engage in activities, especially physical activities (Beck, Davis, & Freeman, 2015). They often encourage the use of antidepressants to assist clients to begin re-engagement.

One difficulty with the CBT approach is the difficulty in getting the depressed client to carry out their homework assignments of engagement. Individuals who suffer depression can be very hard to motivate.

Resource Therapy

Resource Therapy (Emmerson, 2014a) is a therapy that is based on a theory that views personality as segmented in parts, called Resources. One part might want to rest, and another part might want to get work done. One part might want to gamble, and another part might earnestly disapprove of gambling. One part might present to a therapist complaining about what another part does, or feels.

Resource therapists believe there is little value in continuing to engage with the complaining part that presents in therapy to achieve the change a client wants. They engage directly with the part that is pathological to effect change most rapidly.

Neuroscientific research that supports the formulation of Resource States is based on two research findings.

1. Brains grow in weight and potential in direct relation to the amount of stimulation exposure (Rosenzweig, Love & Bennett, 1968).

2. Specific types of stimulation result in the building of neural pathways that reflect abilities directly related to the type of training (Cozolino, 2010). Repeated occurrence of an activity builds a Resource State that, when conscious, exhibits behavior related to that activity.

Resource Therapy and Depression

Depression is viewed by resource therapists as one part of the personality becoming so disappointed in some aspect that is important to it that it actively blocks other parts of the personality from positively engaging. Depression is viewed as both psychological and physiological, because when the body disengages, and does not use energy, there is necessarily a slowing of body systems. Part of the purpose of the therapeutic intervention is to, like CBT, get the client to begin re-engaging to increase the energy levels in the body. This first step in therapy allows the following steps to proceed more quickly and easily.

Unlike most other therapists, resource therapists make sure they are talking with the most appropriate personality part for change. When a CBT therapist works with a client to reframe thinking, the client may be already in a personality part that does not need to change its thinking. What the therapist says to the client may be completely agreed with by the client, because the presenting personality part agrees. It would be like telling a student at the front of the room it is not okay to throw spitballs, when it is a student in the back of the room who is upset and acting out. Resource therapists help the disappointed part of the personality reframe its role in life to help it feel useful, but only after other states have been engaged to begin performing positive activity.

Because Resource therapists hold that a disappointed state actively blocks other states from engaging, it is important to gain permission from the disappointed state for other states to begin engaging positively. The RT steps used in this study to help clients reduce their depression are described in the Methodology section below.

Methodology

A Methods section usually consist of 4 sections in a research article, (1) Participants, (2) Apparatus (or Materials), (3) Design, and (4) Procedure. These sections are normally not designated with a heading, but it is important that information from each is included in some manner.

Participants

You should include enough information about participants so the population is clear to the reader, how the sample was selected along with the selection criteria, and the nature of the sample in terms of age and demographics. The N of the sample and the n's of subgroups is also important to include.

Apparatus

Normally, in a research study you will use a measurement scale. In the study we are illustrating here, that is a depression scale, the Beck Depression Inventory-II (BDI-II). You should include the reliability and validity for any scale you use, if they are available. It is better to choose scales that already have these measures established. If you test the reliability of the measure in your study (a good idea), those results can go in your results section.

Design

You don't normally need to say much about your design. This is different from your procedure. The design in our study was a quasi-experimental pre-test, post-test two group design.

It is the design that will establish the kinds of claims you can make; causal or non-causal. You can educate the reader about this when you define your design.

Procedure

The procedure is the step by step way the study was conducted. This needs to be detailed and clear enough so your study could be replicated.

(See pages 14 and 90 for more information on Methodology)

Twenty research participants (12 women and 8 men, all from a large city) were recruited for this study from a larger group of individuals who had called a free depression clinic (Reengage) seeking assistance. All participants had been assessed in an intake interview to determine their entry to the program. Reengage has a three-month waiting list.

Therefore, we could offer a 4-week treatment to 10 volunteers (6 women and 4 men) who were already at the end of their waiting period, and gain a control group from 10 volunteers (6 women and 4 men) who had 4 weeks before their waiting period was finished. We could finish treatment with our treatment group, prior to the beginning of treatment for the control group.

All participants were assured of confidentiality and volunteered with the understanding that they could drop out of the research at any time (ethical approval was obtained from the University of Exmis NHMRC approved ethics committee). There were no dropouts.

All twenty participants were recruited from callers to Reengage, with a 100 per cent acceptance. We feel this was because nothing was being asked of the participants, other than to take two short Beck Depression Inventory-II scales (Beck, Steer, & Brown, 1996).

The Beck Depression Inventory-II is a 21-item depression scale that is usually completed in 5 to 10 minutes. It has high reliability ratings in the low .90's. It has convergent validity ratings against the Hamilton Psychiatric Rating Scale for Depression (HRSD-R) of .71, and against the Symptom Checklist-90-Revised (SCL-90-R) of .89 (Beck, Steer, & Brown, 1996).

During week 1 of the study all 20 participants were given the Beck Depression Inventory-II as a pre-test. All ten treatment participants began treatment during the first week and their treatment continued for a total of 4 weeks. While there were no dropouts, two participants missed one session each. Their scores were not adjusted in the post-test due to their treatment lasting for only 3 weeks.

At the end of the first 4 weeks of the study all participants, both treatment and control, were given the Beck Depression Inventory-II (post-test) for the second time. At that time, the treatment group had already finished 4 weeks of treatment and the control group had not started their treatment.

The design for this study was a two-group, pre-test, post-test design, where the two groups were not randomly assigned, but they were similar in nature, with the only difference being one group was a month later than the other group on the waiting list. Both groups were pre-tested and post-tested at the same times.

The design was quasi-experimental. Any slight differences in the groups during the pre-test could be statistically accounted for in an Analysis of Covariance (ANCOVA). The quasi-experimental design an excellent design when the two groups are similar enough to have been expected to (without treatment) change similarly over the same period (the four weeks of the study). Results from this design are more generalizable than randomized designs, as the research requires less disturbance to real life settings. By statistically accounting for pre-test differences, the difference in the groups in the post-test can be attributed to the treatment (Dimitrov & Rumrill, 2003).

There was no assessment of change from pre-test to post-test. There did not need to be. The difference assessment was between the control group (those who did not have the treatment) and the treatment group (those who had the RT treatment), to answer the question, "What difference did the treatment make?" Had the assessment been made from pre-test to post-test other factors might have been involve in that change, other than the treatment, such as Maturation, History, Regression toward the mean (Campbell and Stanley, 1971).

The time-line for this study was, as follows.

1. Week 1 – Both groups were given the Beck Depression Inventory-II (pre-test).

2. Week 1 – The treatment started with the treatment group, with 1 hour individual sessions.

3. Weeks 2-4 – Treatment continued with the treatment group, with 1 session per week, totaling 4 sessions.

4. Week 4 – At the end of week 4, both groups were given the Beck Depression Inventory-II a second time (post-test).

5. The two groups were compared using an ANCOVA procedure with the dependent variable being the post-test, the independent variable being treatment group, and the controlled covariate being the pre-test.

The treatment

Below are the RT steps to help reduce depression that were employed in this study, over the 4 sessions with the treatment. The reader should not attempt this procedure without understanding the precise intervention in more depth. These steps are detailed further in Resource Therapy texts (Emmerson, 2014a, 2014b, 2015) and bringing the right Resource State into the conscious has been detailed in the literature (Emmerson, 2016).

1. Rapport was established.

2. Two Resources were located that had previously experienced enjoyment or excitement in an activity where engagement would still be possible for the client.

3. A time when one of these activities was enjoyed was revivified until it was obvious that the client was experiencing a level of joy or excitement within the imagery.

4. A name for that Resource State was negotiated, and that Resource was asked if it would be willing to again engage positively in the activity that it had in the past, if internal permission can be gained.

5. Step three and four was also completed for the second Resource from step two.

6. The Resource that was disappointed (core of the depression) was brought to the conscious and permission was gained from that state for the two Resources to reengage in the activities they have enjoyed in the past. The disappointed state spoke directly to each of the other states to give permission verbally.

7. In the following sessions, work proceeded to ensure positive activities were occurring and with the disappointed state to determine its purpose and find adjusted or new roles where it could continue to fulfil that purpose.

(adapted from Emmerson, 2015, p. 141)

While both CBT and RT encourage the depressed client to begin engaging in positive activities, only RT gains permission from the disappointed state for states to begin engaging. Without gaining permission for engagement to begin from the disappointed state, it can be very difficult for clients to begin positively active behaviors. Clients will often report that they had wanted to 'go on a walk' but they just did not make it happen. The apparent reason for this is that there was a struggle between the state that wanted to walk and the state that was blocking positive activity. By gaining permission from the disappointed state, it makes it much easier for the client to begin re-engaging in positive activities.

The final step in the treatment is also important. The disappointed state needs to learn that, while life may not be like it was, the state is an important part of the personality and it can itself engage in a helpful way. When this state begins seeing a positive role for itself the client most often continues to improve even following the conclusion of therapy sessions.

Results

The Results section should include a summary of the collected data and analyses, which follows from the analytic plan. All results should be described, including unexpected findings. Authors should include both descriptive statistics and tests of significance (American Psychological Association, 2010, p. 8).

(See page 15 for more information on Results sections)

We wanted to determine if Resource Therapy is an effective therapy for depression. Therefore, in conjunction with a quasi-experimental pre-test, post-test, two-group design, we employed an ANCOVA procedure to analyze post-treatment differences between treatment and control groups, while controlling for pre-treatment differences by using the pre-test as a covariate. By controlling for pre-treatment differences, differences in the post-test can be attributed to the treatment. Following a Resource Therapy (RT) treatment, the treatment group (adjusted m=50.16, SE=2.14) had significantly lower levels of depression than did the control group (adjusted m=65.04, SE=2.14), $F(1,17) = 24.02$, $p<.001$. The difference in scores between the Resource Therapy group and the control group accounted for 58.6 percent of the variance (η^2_p) in the depression scores. These results reveal that the Resource Therapy treatment for depression, as applied in this research, can profoundly reduce the depression levels in participants.

Table 1, below, illustrates the differences between the Control and Treatment groups prior to any adjustments for pre-test differences. You can observe the difference in depression levels following the 4-week RT treatment.

Table 1 **Descriptives – Non-Adjusted Depression Means**

Original Non-Adjusted Means	Mean	SD	N
Control Group	64.60	18.98	10
RT Treatment Group	50.60	10.48	10

Table 2 illustrates the differences in depression scores between the Control and Treatment groups after the means have been adjusted for pre-test differences. Here we can observe a similar mean difference as we saw in Table 1.

Table 2 Marginal Means – Adjusted Depression means

	Marginal Mean	SE	Lower CI	Upper CI
Control Group	65.04	2.147	60.51	69.57
RT Treatment Group	50.16	2.147	45.63	54.69

This small change in mean differences, the difference in means prior to controlling for pre-test differences (14) and difference in means after controlling for pre-test differences (14.88), indicates the two groups were quite similar in their depression scores at the beginning of the study. The within group variations did not violate the assumption of equal variances, Levenes $F(1,18) = 1.13$, $p > .05$).

The benefit of controlling for pre-test differences is to ensure that any differences found between the groups following the treatment are not reflective of original differences between the groups at the beginning of the study. The use of the pre-test depression score as a covariate also sensitizes the analysis to determine more precisely the real impact of the treatment (Dimitrov & Rumrill, 2003).

Discussion

"… your discussion, (is) the place where you sew up the various threads of your research into a cohesive narrative. This is not the time to hurry through just because the end is in sight, say experts and students alike. Rather, it's the time to pull back and take a fresh look at your work. … Your discussion should begin with a cogent, one-paragraph summary of the study's key findings, but then go beyond that to put the findings into context, says Stephen Hinshaw, PhD, chair of the psychology department at the University of California, Berkeley" (Azar, 2006, p. 1).

(See page 15 for more information on Discussion sections)

Resource Therapy has been shown to be an effective treatment for depression. With only 4 weeks of RT treatment participants' depression scores were significantly lower than those who did not have the treatment, with the difference in scores between the Resource Therapy group and the control group accounting for 58.6 percent of the variance in the depression scores. Further studies comparing RT to CBT should be able to clarify the preferred treatment for depression.

CBT has been forwarded as the 'therapy of choice' for depression because of research that has shown it to be effective. There is concern related to the CBT research due to the high number of research studies conducted on this therapy. With alpha set at .05, as is normal, there is a 5% chance of a false positive result in any single study. That means that, on average, with every 100 studies on CBT with depression, 5 studies will show false positive results. False positives an issue any time there are large numbers of studies in an area of research, especially when journals are inclined to print only the positive results. It becomes difficult to understand the true efficacy of a treatment when the potential exists for so many false positive results. A large number of potential false positive results does not mean that CBT is an ineffective treatment for depression. It does mean that claims of, 'therapy of choice' need to be evaluated with an awareness of the multiple testing issue.

Considering the results of the present study, these are benefits for the use of Resource Therapy.

1. The efficacy of the Resource Therapy treatment has been demonstrated without combining the treatment with antidepressant medication.

2. The therapeutic technique of gaining internal permission for active personality parts to begin reengaging may make it easier for clients to begin participating in positive activities in a timelier manner.

3. Attention to the forlorn or disappointed personality part (the cause) to ensure that it discovers its purpose and finds a way to engage in fulfilling that purpose, may enhance both the swiftness and the lasting effects of the treatment.

Caution

While the Resource Therapy steps for working with depressed clients have been noted in this article, the reader should not attempt to duplicate these steps without further study. Both books and training in Resource Therapy are available (see resourcetherapyinternational.com). For example, an important action in this therapy is called Vivify Specific (Emmerson, 2016). Vivify Specific is the technique to bring the wanted state into the conscious so it can be spoken with directly. When working with depressed clients, this action is used to bring into the conscious the parts that have engaged in positive activities, and it is also used to bring into the conscious the disappointed state.

It is imperative that the right Resource States are in the conscious at the right times, for RT to have quick and lasting power. RT is distinguished from other therapies in two ways, 1) it ensures that the therapist is speaking with the parts that need change, and 2) it has a structure that fosters a diagnosis and designates a clear set of actions for each diagnosis. Therefore, it is important for those wanting to use Resource Therapy to learn the various diagnoses and the corresponding RT actions.

Limitations

The results of the present study are impressive. With a small sample size, significant differences were found between the RT treatment and the control group. Finding a significance was only possible because of the large effect size of the treatment, 58.6% variance explained.

Because small sample sizes are not as generalizable, they are given a high bar to achieve significance. It is assumed that, even though the sample size was small, the difference was so big we can be at least 95% sure that the result was caused by the treatment. The small sample size is still a limitation of this study. It would have been better to have larger groups, in part to be able to look at efficacy with sub strata, such as gender, age, and depression etiology.

Another limitation was that the groups were not randomly assigned. The most sensitive research for indicating causal relationships are experimental designs with random assignment. Random assignment ensures better equality of the groups at the beginning of the research.

This study ensured equality of the groups with the use of a pre-test. The pre-test was used as a covariate, so pre-test differences were accounted for and statistically removed from the post-test scores. This quasi-experimental design does have a benefit compared to a random assignment design. There is less disruption to participants, therefore there is better generalizability of results. Had participants been placed in a single group then their treatment times manipulated according to the randomly selected group they were place into, normal treatment timetables would have been altered. The design of the present study did not alter normal treatment timetables; therefore, the results are more generalizable to future patients that have those same timetables.

Ethical approval was more straightforward, because no participant was delayed in receiving any treatment. Each participant maintained his or her normal place on the waiting list.

Need for future research

This research is the first study of Resource Therapy in the treatment of depression. There needs to be more, especially with different types of depression, and with different subgroups of participants.

Because Resource Therapy is a new therapy, there is a great need and opportunity for further research. RT appears to show positive results with clients dealing with addiction, with eating disorders, and with PTSD and with other trauma related disorders. There are RT interventions across the range of DSM categories (Emmerson, 2014a). Researchers wanting to contribute to the psychotherapy field can do so by investigating the power of working with the right personality parts in a structured way.

A researcher with a special interest has an opportunity to demonstrate the power of these techniques with multiple studies. For example, a researcher with an interest in anorexia could perform multiple studies using Resource Therapy. That person would become a sought-after expert, able to offer expertise and training in the techniques that have been tested.

Conclusion

A 4-week Resource Therapy treatment resulted in significantly lower depression scores for participants. Anecdotal evidence from RT therapists made it clear that this therapy showed real promise for helping individuals suffering from depression. Together with this evidence and the causal results demonstrated in this study, Resource Therapy provides promise for those suffering from depression.

It is recommended that more therapists learn these techniques and that more researchers investigate RT techniques with other diagnoses.

Chapter 7: Non-experimental and non-research articles

A non-experimental research article reports new research that was done for the study being presented, but the researcher cannot claim the treatment caused any observable change.

Non-research articles are not based on new research. They are articles about theory or practice where there was no study conducted. They often draw on research already published.

Non-experimental articles

We learned in *Chapter 3: Research design* that there are three types of research, experimental, quasi-experimental, and non-experimental. The first two types allow us to say that our treatment caused the observed change in participants, while non-experimental research does not allow those types of claims. Non-experimental includes qualitative research, and research that is not capable of eliminating confounding variables (such as pre-group differences, maturation, history, testing, mortality, and regression toward the mean).

Examples of non-experimental research

1. Research based on correlations: We have learned that just because two things share a relationship, that does not mean one of them causes the other one to change (remember little kids foot sizes and reading ability). It is only a test of difference research that allows causal claims.

2. Survey Research: While surveys can be incorporated into an experimental or quasi-experimental design they most normally are not. Survey research can help describe a population and it can show relationships.

3. Qualitative Research: Qualitative research is powerful research that gives voice to participants so the reader can better understand their experiences. It often builds hypotheses about groups or events, while quantitative research can scientifically test hypotheses. There are many research questions that cannot be answered without

the use of qualitative research. It does not compare groups while holding confounding variables constant.

4. Research where there are statistical comparisons without the elimination of confounding variables: Non-experimental research often has a lot of statistics. A test may be conducted between a pre-test and a post-test to see if a significant difference can be found. Afterward, the researcher will not be able to claim any difference was due to the treatment because other factors could have caused the difference. Likewise, two groups may be compared statistically, such as the happiness of those who had a university education against the happiness of those who did not. Any difference cannot be attributed to the university education, because those who attend university are different than those who do not, and they would necessarily have different levels of happiness even if neither group had attended university.

Non-experimental research does contribute evidence. It just does not contribute the kind of evidence that can support a causal claim. If the scores of participants on a pre-test do not differ significantly following a treatment on a post-test then there is no evidence that the treatment may have helped. If the scores of individuals on a pre-test do differ significantly from the scores of those individuals on a post-test then the treatment may have caused that change. Other things may have caused the change, but a dramatic change after a treatment can be compelling evidence to the reader that the treatment should be tried.

When you can do experimental or quasi-experimental research, do it. It is worth the extra time and effort. When you cannot do causal research, you may be able to do non-experimental research that provides the reader with evidence that is important. If the question is between no research and non-experimental research the preference should be the latter.

Why not just do causal research?

Ethics

You may not be able to incorporate a causal research design into your study because of ethics or logistics. It is not ethical to withhold treatment from a person for research.

Therefore, it may be unethical to have a control group wait for a treatment. If you do not know if the treatment is going to be helpful, then you are not withholding something that has been shown to be beneficial.

(If you have had a waiting control group, then it is ethical to offer them the treatment if it is found to be beneficial, after the treatment group has been compared to the control group. By doing this, you are also able to gather more data to support the benefit of the treatment. The pre-post data of the control group that is offered a later treatment will be non-experimental, but it will be more data to build the case for the efficacy of the treatment.)

Logistics

Logistics is sometimes impossible to overcome. To compare two groups, you really need at least 10 participants in each group to have any chance of finding significance. The higher the N the more chance there is to find a significant difference between two groups. A pre-post evaluation can be done without a need to divide the participants into two groups. This gives more power to find a significance.

It is better to find a significance in a non-experimental design than not to have a finding in a causal design. If you have 15 research participants then you do not have enough to divide into two groups. If you have two groups that you would like to do a pre-test, post-test two group design with, as in the article example above, but one group only has 7 participants in it, then you cannot logistically carry out that design.

Sometimes a researcher works for an organization that is inflexible in allowing any deviation from their procedures. This can preclude a causal research design, but still allow a non-experimental design.

How to report non-experimental research

Non-experimental evidence can be presented to build a case that the treatment was effective. When reporting non-experimental research, you must avoid causal terminology, such as effect, lead to, resulted in, affected, and caused. Make sure your title does not refer to "The effect of" or "The efficacy of".

What you can do is merely report your results and let the reader decide if the case for the treatment is compelling. You can clearly state any significant findings. For example, "There was a significant difference in the anger scores of participants after the treatment, compared to their scores prior to the treatment."

You do not need to be apologetic for your design. Report your findings boldly. Just make sure you do not use causal terms that could be refuted by a reviewer. It is wise to mention in a limitations section inside the discussion that the design of the study was non-experimental. You can add in this section that the results are still compelling. It is appropriate to call for further research to better verify the results.

Structure of a non-experimental report

The structure of a non-experimental report is almost identical to that of a casual study. The only real difference is the claims you make (don't make causal claims or use causal terms), and the need to mention in the limitations section that your study was non-experimental. I have included examples of non-causal results paragraphs in several of the statistical analyses.

In all other ways, follow the suggestions throughout this book. Write your article in a clear fashion, telling the reader the story of your research.

It is easier to get causal research published, but there are many non-experimental research studies in publication.

Non-research articles

That term 'non-research' sounds worse than it is. Many very valuable articles are non-research articles. If you want to present a theory or if you want to explain a technique you have had success with, you may do so in a non-research article. You will not term it non-research. This book is non-research, as it is not reporting new research findings.

The purpose of this book is to encourage research, but I will succinctly address some aspects of writing non-research articles. Non-research articles may address theory, practice, or theory and practice. The main difference in the structure of non-research and research articles is the non-research articles do not have methodology and findings sections. You do not need ethical approval for non-research articles.

Theory articles

A theory article presents either a psychological theory or a way of theorizing psychological issues. Myself and Philipa Thornton have written an article introducing Resource Therapy. It has been submitted and is awaiting blind referee review.

This article defines Resource Therapy and the eight pathologies in the theory. It defines Sensory Experience Memory and the importance it has both in understanding pathology and in therapeutic interventions. The article explains the scientific evidence the theory is drawn from, evidence from other studies. The article describes RT theory in relation to addictions, eating disorders, attachment disorders, and dissociative identity disorder.

There is no attempt in the article to train the reader in a practice technique. There is an attempt to present a new therapy in a way that may encourage others to read and get training in the techniques.

A theory article does not have step by step procedures presented in a way that the reader could immediately begin using with clients. Theory articles provide new ways of looking at psychology.

When writing a theory article, it is appropriate to provide a context, a need, and a utility for the theory that is being presented. It is good to support the theory with references to other research and theory articles.

Practice articles

My article, *The expression, removal and relief method of resolving trauma* (Emmerson, 2004) was a straightforward presentation of how to therapeutically resolve trauma. It is a good example of a practice article. This article was written to provide therapists with a technique they could begin using immediately. It went into the depth needed for them to use the technique.

While there was some introduction to the technique, the main thrust of the article was on practice. Often practice articles will have fewer references. It is still important to provide some context, and to credit others who are working in the area, but the main emphasis is on techniques.

These are very useful articles to advance therapeutic skills. While there are a lot in publication, they will not be published in the better journals as often as research articles.

Articles about therapy practice techniques should be written with the same writing imperatives as other articles. They should begin describing the general area to draw the reader in, and they should move to the specific techniques that are being presented. After detailing the techniques with enough specificity to allow the reader to use them, the article should move back to a more general presentation of the overall benefit the technique will provide in treating clients.

Theory and practice articles

Theory and practice articles are very common. They can also be very useful. They inform the reader about a new theoretical understanding, about its implications to therapy practice, and then they include how the theory in the article is used in practice. They describe a technique, based on the presented theory, in enough detail for the reader to begin practicing that technique.

I recently had an article published entitled, *Sensory experience memory in Resource Therapy* (Emmerson, 2017) that makes a good example of a theory and practice article. It introduced a new theoretical concept of memory called sensory experience memory (SEM). This concept was new because it posited that we have two mutually exclusive types of memories, intellectual memories and emotional memories (SEMs).

It was theorized in this article that PTSD, panic attack, phobias, and many anxieties are caused by SEMs, many of which have become disconnected from the intellectual memories that would necessarily align with them. These two types of memories can become re-connected by bridging from the current problematic emotion to the initial sensitizing event.

Covering this aspect of SEMs in the article was purely theoretical. A further aspect of the theory was connected to therapeutic techniques. Part of the nature of SEMs and intellectual memories is that in the short-term they are connected. Immediately following exposure to an event, the individual will have both the intellectual and SEM memory. The emotion, with an intellectual understanding, lingers for a short period. That is an aspect of SEMs that can be used in therapy to foster cathartic breakthroughs in understanding. Catharsis cannot result purely from an intellectual reframing. Therefore, using SEMs in therapy to bring together emotions and understanding can be powerful.

Techniques for using this aspect of SEMs were described in detail in the article. It was the dual nature of presenting a new theoretical prospective, and presenting practical techniques based on that understanding that made this article a theory *and* practice article.

When you write a theory and practice article it is important that you keep the two parts connected and well balanced.

1. Make sure you include enough theory for the reader to have a good appreciation of your thinking.
2. Make sure you sufficiently connect the theory to practice.
3. Make sure you describe the practice in enough detail so the reader will be able to use it with his or her clients.

You should inform the reader how you will be doing this at the beginning, and you should conclude with an overview of how this was demonstrated at the end of the article. I call it 'framing' when you tell the reader what you will be saying, and then remind the reader about what you have said. It is best not to make this practice too obvious or robotic, but when you have something that is important, it deserves to be framed.

Be heard when you write

Readers hear what is said in a short sentence more than what is said in a long sentence. I'll show you. When you consider all the things that a reader will be reading, and knowing that readers can tire when reading a long sentence and black out, it just makes better sense to use shorter sentences on major points when you want to have a bigger impact. Use a short sentence when you want to be heard.

Read the last two sentences again. They say the same thing. If you don't want to lose an idea in a long sentence, make two sentences. - Long sentences can cause readers to lose concentration (or even consciousness). Use a short sentence when you want to be heard.

I am not saying every sentence should be short. Key points should be in short sentences.

Another key to writing is to write strongly, not tentatively. The first two sentences of this book did not say:

This introductory chapter <u>attempts to</u> explain how this book is laid out and what you <u>may</u> learn from it. It <u>can be</u> a good idea to overview what is going to be covered, so, <u>hopefully,</u> when you read something, you will have <u>a better</u> context of the bigger picture.

Instead the first two sentences read:

This introductory chapter explains how this book is laid out and what you can expect to learn from it. It is good to get an overview of what you are going to learn, so everything you read has a context on that big picture.

The underlined words above are tentative words. Some writers are prone to using qualifying, tentative words too much. Don't over speak, but write with conviction. Avoid tentative words.

Headings and first sentences

A final way to emphasize your writing is to use headings and subheadings to spotlight your topic. It is easier for a reader to remember something if they already know the topic.

Each first sentence in a new paragraph should tell the reader the topic of the paragraph. Following sentences should give more detail about the topic introduced in the first sentence. When a new topic is started, a new paragraph should be started.

All articles follow similar conventions

The writing of theory and practice articles follows the same conventions as writing other types of articles. Editors will make clear what is expected in the detailed information they provide to contributors. Make sure the journal you send your article to accepts the type of article you have written.

Chapter 8: How to build a career

The machine

There is a machine happening out there. It was there before you were born and it will evolve and remain after you are gone. Building a career is fitting into that machine in a way that fits you; in a way that advances your contribution and your career. There may be places and times you do not want to fit into the machine, but unless there are places and times that you can, then you will not be heard.

This book is, in part, about the rules of that machine. You will need to follow those rules, in ethics, in formatting, and in analysis if you want to be published. The better you learn those rules the more successful you can be.

Your time will have been well spent it you read about the editor of the journal where you want to send your article. When Churchill met Stalin at Yalta he did not go without knowing everything he could about the man who he was going to met. He needed to know how Stalin thought, what he might agree to, and what he might not. It pays to be informed.

Be informed. Before you send an article to a journal, look at the kinds of articles that journal is already printing, and find out what the editor is interested in, what drives him or her. Present your article, especially your cover letter, in a way that provides the best path to acceptance.

One common thing that drives most editors is the desire to publish articles that will be referenced by others. The scoresheet in professional journals is the number of times a journal is referenced in other articles. Knowing that, it is good to make a case in the cover letter why your article will be of interest to others who will reference it.

Write in a way that fits nicely into the publication machine, but don't compromise your integrity. I once had an article accepted by a good journal, but was told I would need to take a reference out, because the article I was referencing was written by a 'lay author'. A suggestion was made to me for a different person I could reference. I responded that the person I referenced was the original author of the idea. It was his professional property, and he should get credit for it, not someone with a professional degree who had talked about it later. The editor said it was the policy of the journal not to publish articles that referenced lay authors. When I sent the article for consideration it was formatted and generally written to follow the rules of the machine. There was just one rule I could not obey. I withdrew my article from consideration and had it published in a different journal.

A focused career

You go into a large auditorium to see a play. Which light most focuses your attention, 5 bulbs or a single spotlight? Obviously, the spotlight has the most impact.

Focus is important both in a single article, and in a career. When you write an article, don't try to say too much. Keep it focused. Let everything you say illuminate your finding, and your finding will be better heard and remembered by the readers. Let there be spotlights shining on a single finding and it will be illuminated the most brightly.

This same 'spotlight' idea holds true for your career. Write 5 articles about 5 different topics and your career will not be spotlighted. Write 5 articles about different aspects of addiction, and you will become the expert on addiction. It will become easier for you to be published on addiction, you will be asked to speak on addiction, and what you say will be remembered more. Additionally, making conference presentations and books in your expert area would provide a major contribution to the field.

A key is to be interested in what you do. If you care about addiction, and really want to help people who suffer from it, it will be a pleasure to work in that area and make contributions.

Think outward

Your first focus should be on how you want to change the world. What do you want others to learn? When you write, think about the person who will be reading what you write, and your writing will come easier and it will be clearer.

The words of a self-focused person are not clear. The self-focused person is not thinking about the reader or the contribution, but is thinking about self. It is hard to ride a bike while looking at the peddles. Things happen when you look outside yourself and down the road to what you want changed.

It is best to first think about what you want to contribute, and secondly, to think about your career. Vision and creativity comes from a mind focusing outside oneself. I doubt Einstein was concerned about his career when he contributed so vastly to physics. Give yourself the gift of finding what interests you, and develop it. Think about how it can be used and about what the reader can hear. There is meaning in contribution, both for the reader and for the writer.

Appendix 1: An ANOVA with 3 means

An ANOVA can compare 2 or more means. Therefore, it can be used to compare three treatments, such as Therapy 1, Resource Therapy, and Therapy 3. If you want to work along with the example, the data used here can be downloaded at:

```
https://www.dropbox.com/s/tn9dfcdb4hzyza4/ANOVAANCOVA3means
.txt?dl=0
```

The first step is to click Common/ANOVA/ANOVA, as illustrated below.

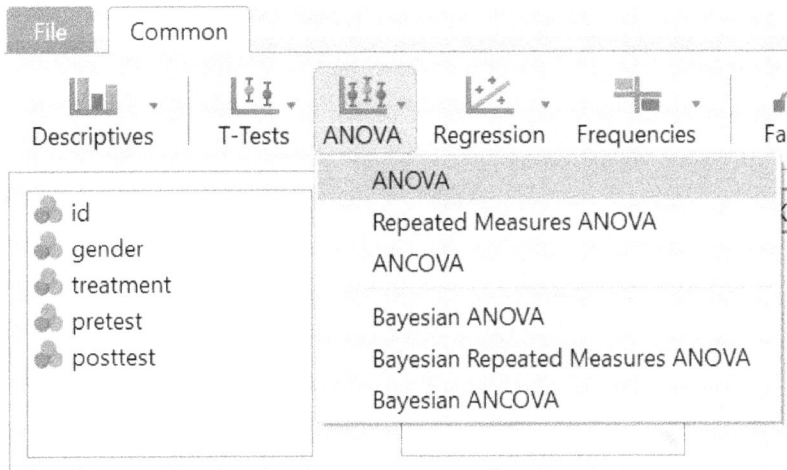

Figure 43: How to select an ANOVA to run

The next steps are to:

1) Put your dependent and independent variables into the equation. In this case, they are post-test and treatment, respectively (see *Figure 44* below).

Because we have more than two groups we will need a post hoc.

2) Under Post Hoc Tests, move 'treatment' to the window on the right and make sure Tukey is ticked. Tukey Post Hoc is a test to see exactly which groups significantly differ, if any. Tukey is the best post hoc to run, in most cases. If your group numbers are very different (one will divide into another more than twice), then select Scheffe, rather than Tukey.

3) At the bottom, under Additional Options, tick Descriptive Statistics, Estimates of effect size, and eta squared (η^2).

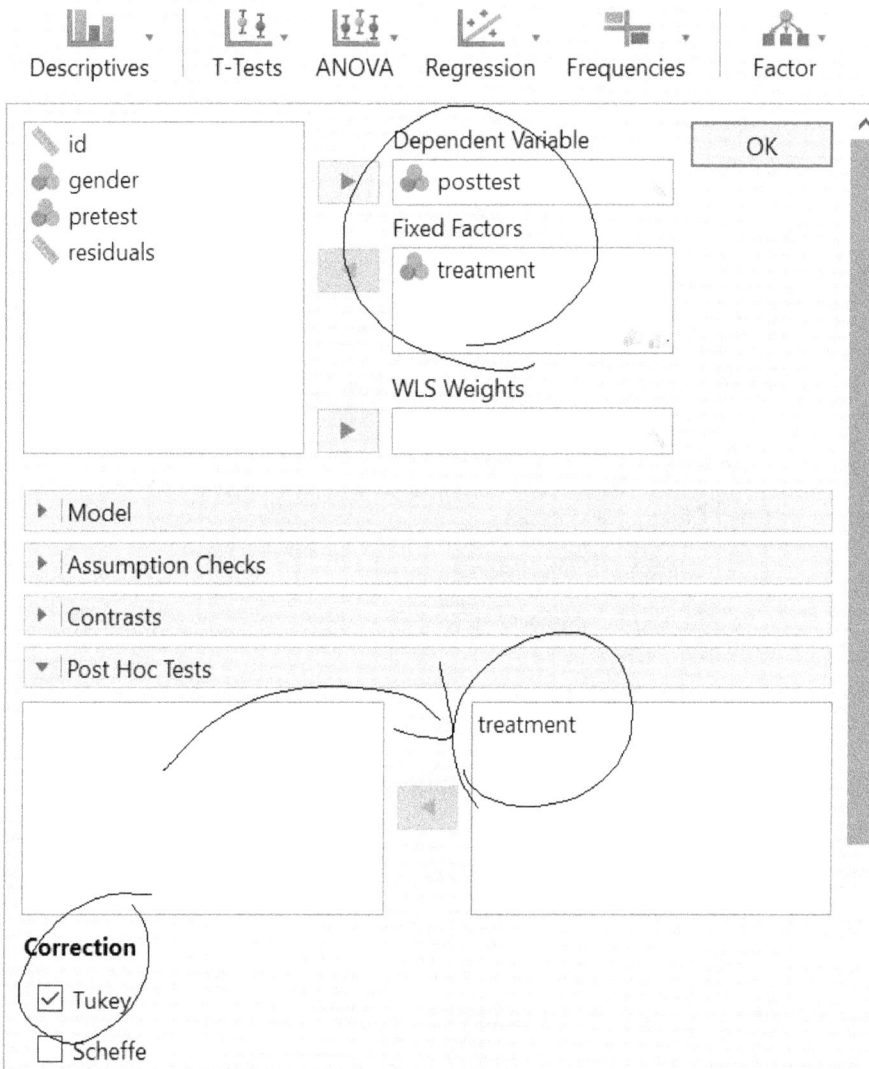

Figure 44: How to set up an ANOVA with more than 2 groups

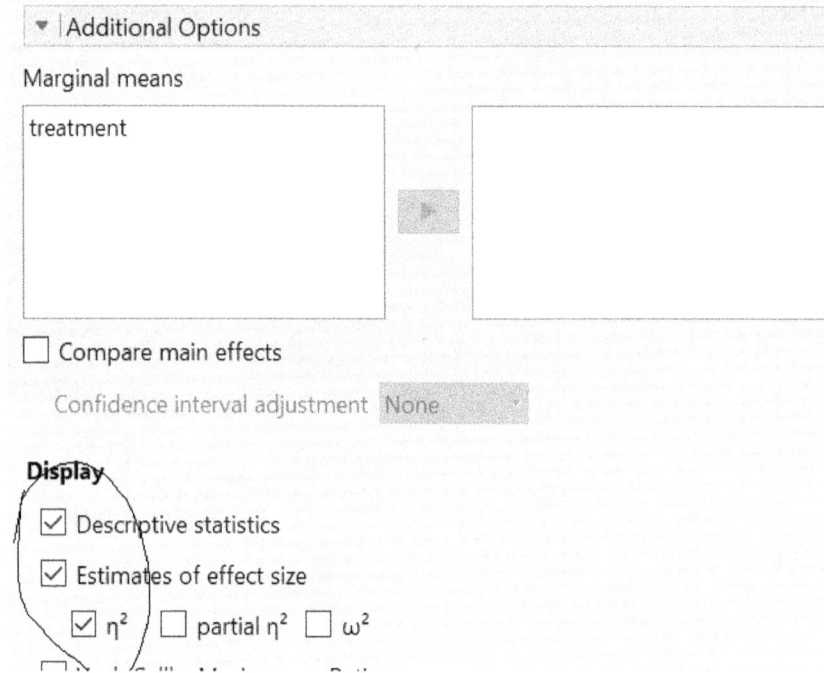

Figure 45: How to get means and effect size

These selections will result in the output below.

The first table, the ANOVA table, provides us with the information to report the F statistic, the significance and the effect size. The APA syntax to report the F statistic and the significance is, $F(2,57) = 2.90$, p<.05.

The η^2 indicates that the differences among the independent variables accounted for 12% of the variance in depression.

The Post Hoc table informs us that there was a significate difference in the depression scores of Treatment 1 and Resource Therapy (p<.05), but there was not a significant difference between Treatment 3 and either of the other two therapies.

The Descriptives Table provides the means, standard deviation and the n's for each group. Any of these tables may be included in the results section of your report if you feel they will clarify the results to the readers.

ANOVA

ANOVA - posttest

Cases	Sum of Squares	df	Mean Square	F	p	η²
treatment	1871	2	935.5	3.902	0.026	0.120
Residual	13667	57	239.8			

Note. Type III Sum of Squares

Post Hoc Tests

Post Hoc Comparisons - treatment

		Mean Difference	SE	t	Ptukey
1	2	14.044	5.031	2.792	0.019
	3	7.055	4.784	1.475	0.310
2	3	−6.990	4.921	−1.420	0.337

Descriptives

Descriptives - posttest

treatment	Mean	SD	N
1	64.60	18.47	20
2	50.56	10.78	18
3	57.55	15.74	22

Figure 46: What to report from an ANOVA with three groups

An example of a results paragraph for this output follows.

We wanted to determine the best intervention for depression, considering Therapy 1, Resource Therapy (RT), and Therapy 3. To do this we randomly divided our sample into three groups and conducted an ANOVA procedure. The ANOVA revealed a significant result, $F(2,57) = 2.90$, $\underline{p}<.05$, with 12% of the variance in depression accounted for by treatment differences. We found that following the therapy interventions, participants who had Resource Therapy (M=50.56) had significantly lower levels of depression than participants who had Therapy 1 (M=64.60).

Depression Levels

treatment	Mean	SD	N
Therapy 1	64.60	18.47	20
Resource Therapy	50.56	10.78	18
Therapy 3	57.55	15.74	22

No significant differences were found between Therapy 3 and either of the other two therapies. Resource Therapy provided better results for those with depression than did Therapy 1, and it appears that RT may be the best treatment choice for depression.

Figure 47: Reporting an ANOVA with three levels

The study reported above was causal, because the sample was randomly divided into treatment groups. There was not a pretest, but the random assignment ensured that the three groups started out equal, so it was not necessary to have a pretest. It would have made the design more sensitive, but it was not necessary to claim causal effects. Because there was random assignment this was an experimental design.

Therefore, we could definitively say that RT provided better results than Therapy 1, because there was a significant difference between these two therapies in relation to the depression levels of participants. Because there was not a significant difference between RT and Therapy 3, we could not say that it provided better results than Therapy 3, even though participants who had RT had lower levels of depression.

Appendix 2: An ANCOVA with 3 means

The ANCOVA is the preferred procedure for the pre-test, post-test, two group design. It adds power (the ability to find a result) to the analysis, and appropriately removes pre-test differences in the groups statistically so the impact of the treatment becomes clear. If a significance is found, it enables the researcher to attribute that improvement directly to the treatment. If you want to work along with the example, the data used here can be downloaded at:

https://www.dropbox.com/s/tn9dfcdb4hzyza4/ANOVAANCOVA3mea ns.txt?dl=0. This is the same data that was used in the last analysis.

I will run the same comparison we ran for the ANOVA procedure, but I will add the pre-test as a covariate, thus removing pre-test differences. Under the Common Tab Select ANOVA/ANCOVA.

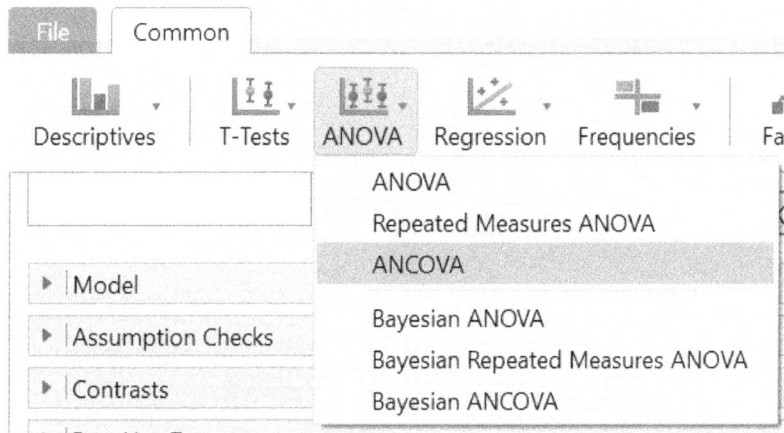

Figure 48: How to select an ANCOVA to run

The next steps are to:

1) put your dependent, independent variable, and your covariate into the equation. In this case, they are post-test, treatment, and pre-test respectively (see *Figure 49* below).

Because we have more than two groups we will need a post hoc.

2) Under Post Hoc Tests, move 'treatment' to the window on the right and make sure Tukey is ticked. The Tukey Post Hoc is a test to see exactly which groups significantly differ, if any. Tukey is the best post hoc to run for independent samples, in most cases. If your group numbers are very different (when one will divide into another more than twice), then select Scheffe, rather than Tukey.

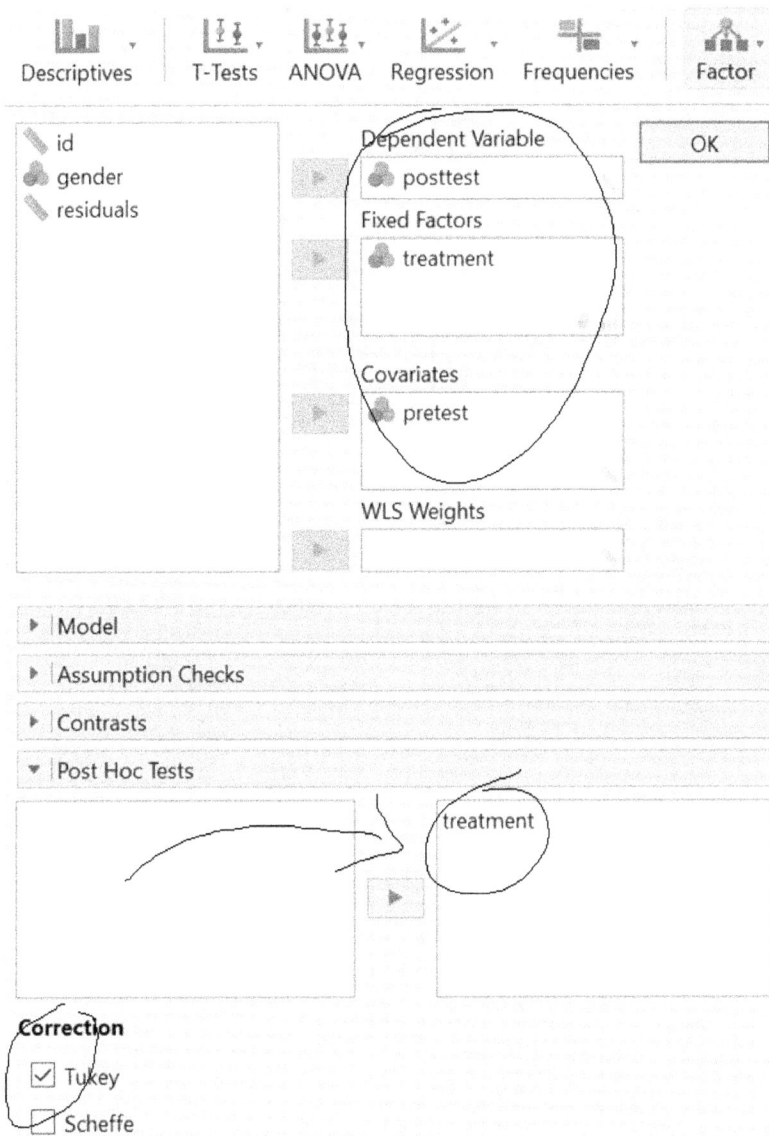

Figure 49: How to run an ANCOVA with three groups

3) At the bottom, under Additional Options, to get the adjusted marginal means, under Marginal means, move treatment from the window on the left to the window on the right. Tick Estimates of effect size, and partial eta squared (η^2_p). We do not need to tick Descriptive statistics, because we will be reporting our adjusted marginal means. We do not need η^2, as this would be the variance explained by the treatment prior to removing pre-test differences.

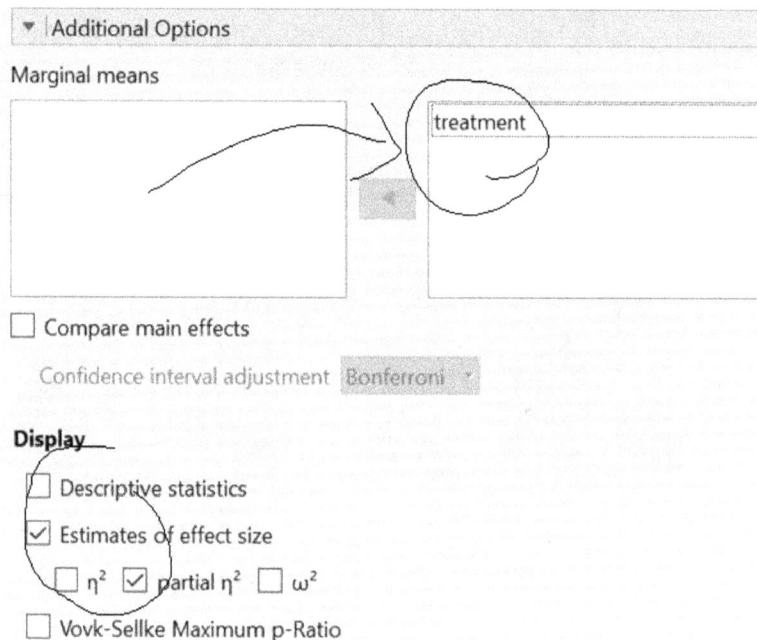

Figure 50: How to get means and effect size

These selections will result in the output below.

The first table, the ANCOVA table, provides us with the information to report the F statistic, the significance and the effect size. The APA syntax to report the F statistic and the significance is, $F_{(2,56)} = 14.06$, $p<.05$.

The η^2_p indicates that the differences among the independent variables accounted for 33.4% of the variance in depression. This effect size is higher than the 12% variance explained in the ANOVA above because the pretest differences have been removed, sensitizing the statistic to better reveal the effect of the treatment.

The Post Hoc table informs us that there was a significate difference in the depression scores of Treatment 1 and Resource Therapy ($p<.05$), and Treatment 1 and Treatment 3, but there was not a significant difference between Resource Therapy and Treatment 3.

The Descriptives Table provides the adjusted, marginal means. These are the means after they have been adjusted for the removal of the influence of the covariate (pre-test). Any of these tables may be included in the results section of your report if you feel they will clarify the results to the readers

ANCOVA ▾

ANCOVA - posttest

Cases	Sum of Squares	df	Mean Square	F	p	η²
treatment	1777	2	888.52	14.06	< .001	0.334
pretest	10127	1	10126.64	160.19	< .001	0.741
Residual	3540	56	63.22			

Note. Type III Sum of Squares

Post Hoc Tests ▾

Post Hoc Comparisons - treatment ▾

		Mean Difference	SE	t	p_tukey
1	2	13.360	2.584	5.171	< .001
	3	8.816	2.460	3.583	0.002
2	3	−4.544	2.534	−1.793	0.181

Marginal Means

Marginal Means - treatment

treatment	Marginal Mean	SE	Lower CI	Upper CI
1	65.04	1.778	60.65	69.43
2	51.68	1.876	47.05	56.31
3	56.22	1.698	52.03	60.42

Figure 51: What to report from an ANCOVA with three groups

The Marginal Means table shows the means, after they have been adjusted following controlling for pre-test differences. These are the means we will be reporting, either in text or in a table.

We wanted to determine the best intervention for depression, considering Therapy 1, Resource Therapy (RT), and Therapy 3. To do this we utilized a two-group, pre-test, post-test design and employed an ANCOVA procedure with the post-test as the dependent variable and the pre-test as the covariate. The ANCOVA revealed a significant result, $F(2,56) = 14.06$, $p<.05$. We found, using a Tukey Post Hoc, that participants who had either Resource Therapy or Therapy 3 had significantly lower levels of depression than participants who had Therapy 1.

Table 1: Marginal Means - Depression Treatment

treatment	Marginal Mean	SE	Lower CI	Upper CI
Therapy 1	65.04	1.778	60.65	69.43
Resource Therapy	51.68	1.876	47.05	56.31
Therapy 3	56.22	1.698	52.03	60.42

Resource Therapy and Therapy 3 provided better results for those with depression than did Therapy 1. No significant difference was found between Resource Therapy and Therapy 3. A larger sample is needed to better determine if Resource Therapy provides significantly better results than Therapy 3 for those with depression.

Figure 52: Reporting an ANCOVA with 3 means

Appendix 3: A repeated measures ANOVA with 3 means

A Repeated Measures ANOVA can compare 2 or more means. Therefore, it can be used to compare a score over three testings, such as pre-treatment depression, post-treatment depression, and one-year follow-up depression. If you want to work along with the example, the data used here can be downloaded at:

https://www.dropbox.com/s/squunvx8mxntx17/RelibilityRepeatedAN
OVA.txt?dl=0

Under the Common Tab Select ANOVA/Repeated Measures ANOVA.

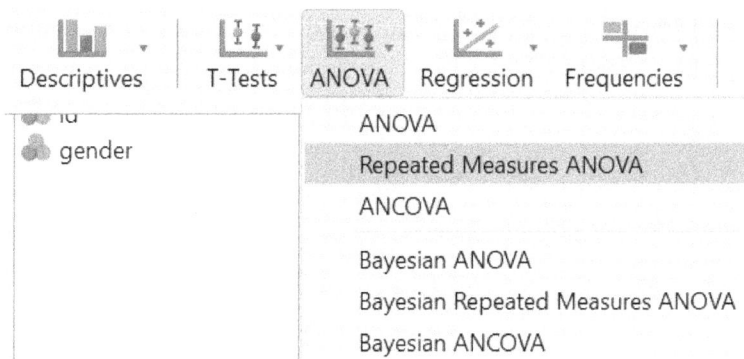

Figure 53: Selecting Repeated Measures ANOVA to run

First click on RM Factor 1 and place there the name of whatever you want to call your independent variable (see *Figure 54* below). In this example, I typed 'Change' there, but another good choice would have been Depression. Then click on Level 1, Level 2, etc. for each mean you are comparing. In this example, I am comparing three means, Pre-test, Post-test, and Follow-up. All means must be on the same scale. You can name them whatever you like. What you name them will appear in the output.

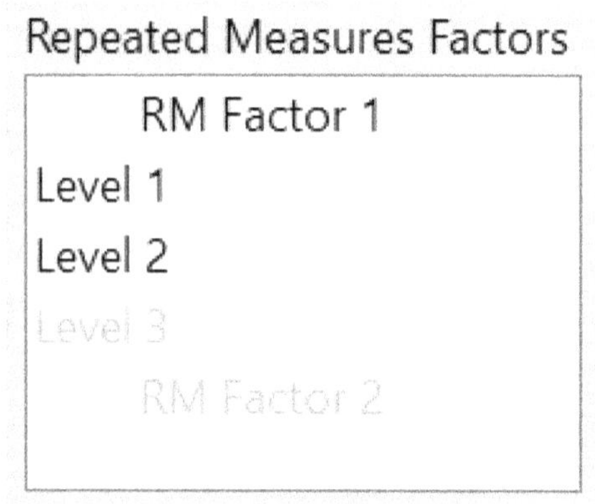

Repeated Measures Factors

RM Factor 1

Level 1

Level 2

Level 3

RM Factor 2

Figure 54: Defining RM Factor 1

You can see below in the first circled area how I have named these (see *Figure 55* below). Next you need to click on the corresponding variables from your variable list and move them over to the Repeated Measures Cells window. Your variables will show up in the left column and the names you have chosen for the output (in the Repeated Measures Factors window) will show up in the right column.

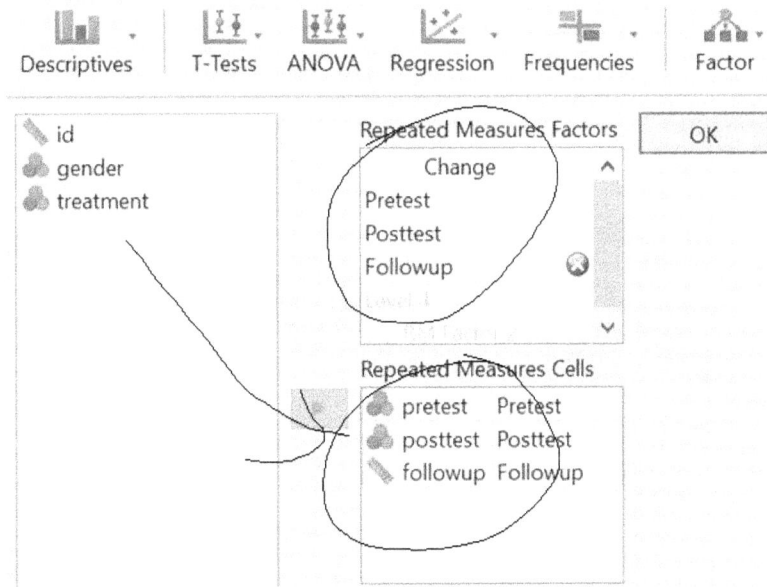

Figure 55: How to run a Repeated Measures ANOVA

Because we are comparing more than two means we will need a post hoc to tell us exactly which means differ significantly. When we compared only two means it was obvious which means differed. Under Post Hoc Tests move your variable (in my example 'Change') from the left window to the right window and make sure Bonferroni is ticked (see *Figure 56* below). A Bonferroni Post Hoc is the preferred test for repeated factors.

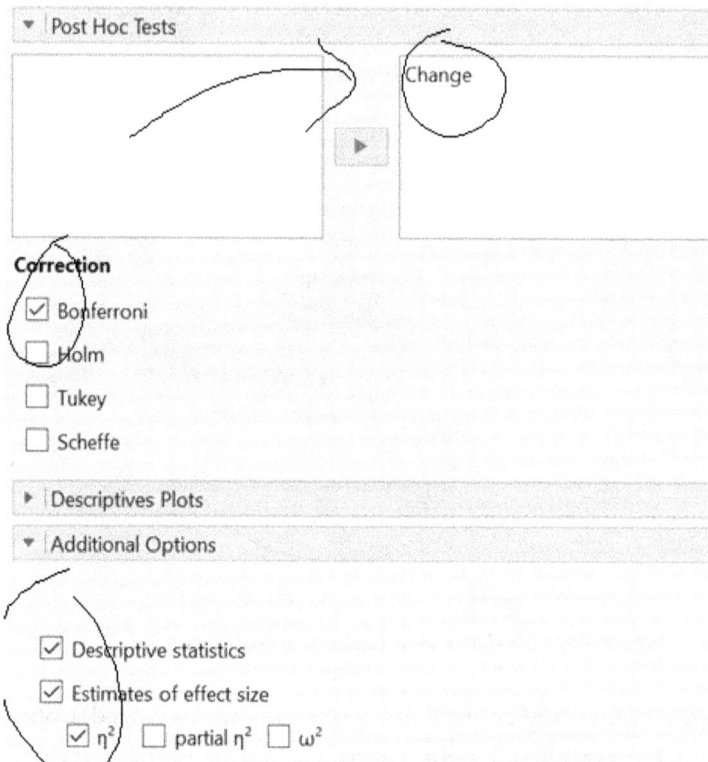

Figure 56: Selecting Post Hoc, means and effect size

Under Additional Options, at the bottom, tick Descriptive statistics to get the means, and Estimates of effect size to get η^2, the variance explained.

These selections will result in the output below.

The first table, the ANOVA table (see *Figure 57*), provides us with the information to report the F statistic, the significance and the effect size. The APA syntax to report the F statistic and the significance is, $F(2,118) = 27.81$, $p<.05$.

The η^2 indicates that the differences among the repeated variables accounted for 32% of the variance in the depression scores.

The Post Hoc table informs us that there was a significate difference in the depression scores between Pre-test, and both Post-test and Follow-up ($p<.05$), and there was not a significant difference between Post-test and Follow-up.

The Descriptives Table provides the means, standard deviation and the n's for each group. Any of these tables may be included in the results section of your report if you feel they will clarify the results to the readers.

Repeated Measures ANOVA

Within Subjects Effects

	Sum of Squares	df	Mean Square	F	p	η²
Change	1600[a]	2[a]	800.02[a]	27.81[a]	< .001[a]	0.320
Residual	3394	118	28.77			

Note. Type III Sum of Squares
[a] Mauchly's test of sphericity indicates that the assumption of sphericity is violated (p < .05).

Post Hoc Tests

Post Hoc Comparisons - Change

		Mean Difference	SE	t	p_{bonf}
Pretest	Posttest	6.700	1.247	5.375	< .001
	Followup	5.867	1.085	5.408	< .001
Posttest	Followup	−0.833	0.382	−2.182	0.099

Descriptives

Descriptives

Change	Mean	SD	N
Pretest	64.50	14.93	60
Posttest	57.80	16.23	60
Followup	58.63	14.91	60

Figure 57: Output for Repeated Measures ANOVA with 3 Means

As with the paired t-test, this procedure does not provide us with a causal result, unless it is analyzing results from a time-series design (see page 25). Therefore, we are limited with the comments we can make regarding the change and its relationship to the Research Therapy treatment.

We wanted to determine if there were significant differences among the depression pre-test scores, depression post-test scores, and the depression one year follow-up scores, following a Resource Therapy treatment. To do this we employed a Repeated Measures ANOVA. A significant reduction in depression was observed following the Resource Therapy intervention, from pre-test (m=64.50, SD=14.93) to post-test (m=57.80, SD=16.23) scores, $F_{(2,118)} = 27.81$, $p<.05$. The one year depression follow-up scores (m=58.63) were also significantly lower than the pre-treatment scores. The η^2 of .32 indicates that 32 percent of the variance from pre-test to post-test is explained by the Resource Therapy treatment. It appears that Resource Therapy is a promising intervention for depression, with this study revealing significantly lower depression scores both immediately following treatment and one year following treatment.

Table 2: Group Descriptives

Depression	Mean	SD	N
Pre-test	64.50	14.93	60
Post-test	57.80	16.23	60
Follow-up	58.63	14.91	60

Figure 58: How to report a Repeated Measures ANOVA with 3 Means

This results paragraph does not have causal claims that were appropriate in the ANCOVA report (i.e., These results reveal that the Resource Therapy treatment for depression profoundly reduced the depression levels in participants). Because this single group repeated design is not a causal design the best we can do is refer to the therapy as promising, rather than 'changing'. Even though this design was not causal, the results still indicate that a change was observed.

Appendix 4: Simple regression

A simple regression is a bit like a Pearson's Correlation. Both have only two variables. The r^2 (variance explained) you can get from squaring a Pearson's is identical to the R^2 you get from a simple regression. If you want to work along with the example, the data used here can be downloaded at:

https://www.dropbox.com/s/78bbezgi5mc3r8o/Regressions.txt?dl=0

In a Pearson's you make no nomination as to dependent and independent variables. You merely put two variables into the analysis. In a simple regression, you must nominate one variable as a dependent variable and one variable as an independent variable.

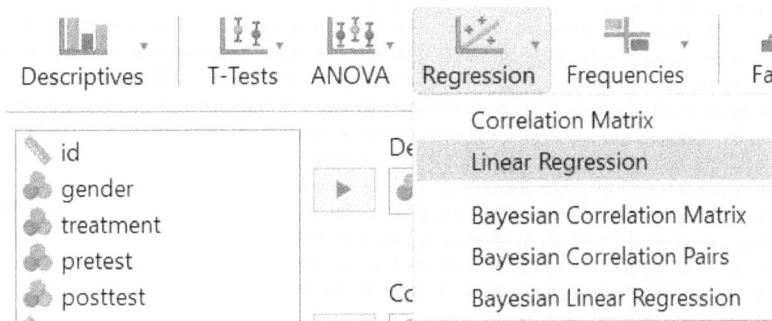

Figure 59: How to select a Regression Procedure

A simple regression procedure provides you with some information that a Pearson's does not. A regression procedure gives you adjusted R^2, a reduced figure for smaller sample sizes. With larger N's the difference between R^2 and adjusted R^2 becomes very small. Generally, if you have over 30 participants you can report R^2 and if you have fewer, then report adjusted R^2.

A regression procedure also gives you the numbers you would need if you want to make a prediction. Given the value of an independent variable you can predict the value of a dependent variable, with the accuracy of the prediction increasing as the correlation between the variables increases. For example, if you wanted to predict happiness, given general mental health, you would be able to get a formula to make that prediction from a simple regression.

By having both general mental health scores and happiness scores for a group, a simple regression can provide you with a prediction formula for the next group of people, when you only have general mental health scores. You could then use those scores to predict their happiness.

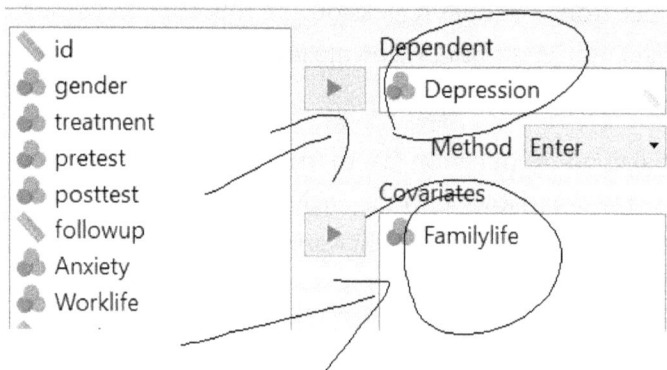

Figure 60: How to set up a Simple Regression

To set up a simple regression you click on the dependent variable (depression) and move it to the top right window (see *Figure 60* above). Then, you click on the independent, predictor variable, and move it to the larger window on the right. There is no need to select an entry selection method, as there is only one independent variable.

The output, below, is not hard to interpret. The R^2 value in the model summary table is the amount of variance in the dependent variable that is explained by the independent variable. The degrees of freedom, the F, and the p value go into the results statement in the same way they do in an ANOVA, $F(1,58) = 16.74$, $p<.05$.

The coefficients table at the bottom of the output is where the regression formula comes from, should you want to use it to predict in the future. You use the unstandardized column to create this formula, Predicted Depression = (Family life score * -0.713) + 68.882. Most people who run regressions are more interested in variance explained, and are not interested in the regression formula.

Should you want to calculate confidence intervals around your prediction you can request those under the statistics pull-down.

Linear Regression ▾

Model Summary

Model	R	R²	Adjusted R²	RMSE
1	0.473	0.224	0.211	12.915

ANOVA ▾

Model		Sum of Squares	df	Mean Square	F	p
1	Regression	2792	1	2791.9	16.74	< .001
	Residual	9675	58	166.8		
	Total	12467	59			

Coefficients

Model		Unstandardized	Standard Error	Standardized	t	p
1	Intercept	68.882	7.742		8.897	< .001
	Familylife	−0.713	0.174	−0.473	−4.091	< .001

Figure 61: How to interpret a Simple Regression

Below is a results paragraph to illustrate how a simple regression may be reported.

> We wanted to determine the amount of variance in depression scores that were explained by family life scores. To do this we employed a simple regression procedure. Family life explained a significant amount of the variance in depression (R^2 = .224), $F(1,58)$ = 16.74, p<.05. Given that 22.4% of the variance in depression was explained by family life scores, it appears that there is a strong relationship between what happens at home and depression.

Regression scores are based on correlations, rather than on experimental design. Therefore, the results are not causal. When there is a relationship we know that relationship could be a causal one, or it could be spurious. It takes causal research design to be able to establish causal relationships.

Appendix 5: Multiple regression

Like Simple Regression, above, Multiple Regression is only included here in an appendix because it is not a statistic that would result in demonstrating a causal relationship. It cannot show that a therapy can create change. If you want to work along with the example, the data used here can be downloaded at:

https://www.dropbox.com/s/78bbezgi5mc3r8o/Regressions.txt?dl=0.
This is the same data that was used in the last analysis. I am including multiple regression here because it may be used to support theory, either in a theoretical article, or as an adjunct part of a causal research article.

If you gain a good understanding of multiple regression it will further help you understand ANCOVA, as both these statistics work with residual variance (see page 46) following the removal of explained variance (see Variance explained, page 38).

Multiple regression may be used to assess the combined amount of variance explained in a dependent variable by a set of independent variables (covariates). For example, we might want to determine the amount of variance in depression that can be explained by family life, work life, and general anxiety.

A multiple regression also provides the numbers for a prediction formula, where a dependent variable might be predicted by a set of independent variables.

When we run a multiple regression, we must select an entry procedure. The selections for entry procedures in JASP are ENTER, FORWARD, BACKWARD, and STEPWISE. ENTER enters all variables with no exclusion for non-significant variables, so we would not use it past an initial exploration stage when we have more than one predicter. I will explain and demonstrate a Forward Regression and then briefly mention Backward and Stepwise Regressions.

The first step is to click Common/Regression/Linear regression.

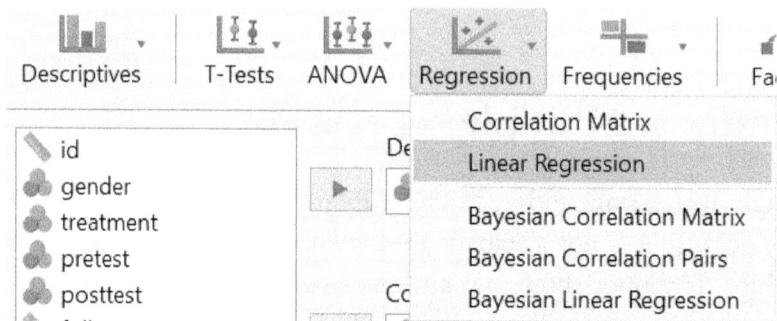

Figure 62: How to select a Regression Procedure

To run a forward regression, select the dependent variable (Depression) and move it to the top window (see *Figure 63* below). From the pulldown select the Forward procedure. Next, select the independent variables (here called covariates) and move them into the Covariates window. It does not matter what order they are selected.

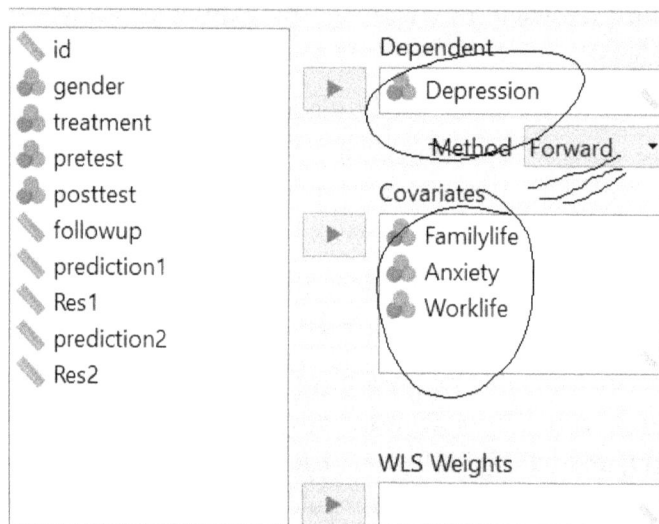

Figure 63: How to set up a Forward Multiple Regression

The results from these selections can be seen below. There is a lot in these results, and it is important for us to look at them closely to understand them. To help clarify these results I have also run a series of correlations in the figures below.

Linear Regression ▼

Model Summary

Model	R	R²	Adjusted R²	RMSE
1	0.473	0.224	0.211	12.915
2	0.571	0.326	0.302	12.144

ANOVA

Model		Sum of Squares	df	Mean Square	F	p
1	Regression	2792	1	2791.9	16.74	< .001
	Residual	9675	58	166.8		
	Total	12467	59			
2	Regression	4061	2	2030.5	13.77	< .001
	Residual	8406	57	147.5		
	Total	12467	59			

Coefficients ▼

Model		Unstandardized	Standard Error	Standardized	t	p
1	intercept	68.882	7.742		8.897	< .001
	Familylife	−0.713	0.174	−0.473	−4.091	< .001
2	intercept	80.667	8.315		9.702	< .001
	Familylife	−0.535	0.175	−0.355	−3.058	0.003
	Worklife	−0.333	0.114	−0.340	−2.933	0.005

Figure 64: How to interpret a Multiple Regression

Let's look at the regression results above before looking at the correlation matrices. The first table is the model summary, and the most important statistics in this table are the R^2 numbers. This table indicates that two significant variables have come into the equation to estimate the total amount of variance that can be explained by the set of independent variables.

Line one of the 'model summary' table indicates that when the first independent variable was entered into the equation, 22.4% of the variance in depression was explained by it. The numeral 1 indicates that this was the first step in the regression procedure. When we look at the Coefficients table we can tell that the first step in the procedure entered Family life into the equation.

Therefore, it was Family Life that explained 22.4% of the variance in depression. That is equal to all the variance in depression that was explained by family life.

This step was accomplished by the regression procedure, internally, by running a correlation between depression and all the independent variables, then choosing the variable that shared the highest correlation with depression. In this case that was family life, and this can be seen by looking at the correlation matrix directly below.

Family life had the strongest correlation with depression, -0.473. This correlation squared is .224, the same as the R^2 for family life in the regression model summary. Because family life correlated with depression the strongest, it was the first variable to enter the equation. Had it not correlated significantly with depression it would not have entered, and there would have been no regression solution.

We can also see in the correlation matrix below that work life correlated with depression significantly with a correlation of -0.464. This variable explained 21.5% of the variance in depression on its own (-0.464^2), but we will never see this number coming out of the regression procedure. The reason for that will be made clear below.

Predictions

The unstandardized column in the coefficients table in the regression output has the numbers needed to predict depression levels at each step in the procedure. For example, if we wanted to predict depression with only family life we could make the regression formula, predicted depression = (family life * -0.713) + 68.882. The first residuals (Res1) that are correlated against the independent variables in the second step of the procedure will be each person's actual depression score minus this predicted depression score.

The regression formula following the entry of the second variable (work life) will be, predicted depression score = (family life * -0.535) + (work life * -0.333) + 80.667. When this predicted depression score is subtracted from the actual depression scores of individuals the second set of residuals is the result.

We can see this Res2 variable in the correlation matrix in *Figure 68*, below. To calculate Res1 and Res2 for the illustrative correlation matrices (*Figure 67* and

Figure 68) I put these formulas in the Excel spreadsheets, then I ran the corresponding correlations with the Res1 and Res2 variables from the calculations (see *Figure 31:* Calculating residuals in EXCEL, page 73).

Correlation Matrix

Pearson Correlations

		Anxiety	Worklife	Familylife	Depression
Anxiety	Pearson's r	—	0.715	−0.124	−0.234
	p-value	—	< .001	0.347	0.072
Worklife	Pearson's r		—	0.348	−0.464
	p-value		—	0.006	< .001
Familylife	Pearson's r			—	−0.473
	p-value			—	< .001
Depression	Pearson's r				—
	p-value				—

Figure 65: The initial correlation matrix

After the first step in the regression procedure the variance shared by depression and family life (black area in *Figure 66*) is removed, leaving only the residual variance in depression (light grey area in *Figure 66*) that will have no relationship with the differences in family life scores (the covariate).

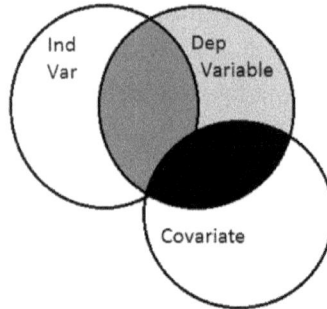

Figure 66: Removing covariance, leaving residual variance

The next correlation matrix, below, illustrates the second step in the regression procedure. All independent variables are correlated to the residual variance in depression, after the variance that was explained by family life has been removed.

Notice that family life does not correlate with this residual variance at all. The reason for this is because all the variance it shared with depression has already been accounted for, and removed. Also notice that the correlations of work life and anxiety have changed.

Work life now correlates with the residual variance -0.34, explaining 11.6% of this variance. Remember, it did explain 21.5% of the variance in depression by itself, but when the variance that family life explained was removed, almost 10% of the variance that work life explained went with it.

Correlation Matrix

Pearson Correlations

		Anxiety	Worklife	Familylife	Res1
Anxiety	Pearson's r	—	0.715	−0.124	−0.332
	p-value	—	< .001	0.347	0.010
Worklife	Pearson's r		—	0.348	−0.340
	p-value		—	0.006	0.008
Familylife	Pearson's r			—	0.000
	p-value			—	1.000
Res1	Pearson's r				—
	p-value				—

Figure 67: Correlations with depression residuals after removal of family life covariance

While both work life and anxiety now explain a significant amount of the variance in the residuals, work life explains the most so it is the next variable to go into the equation. You can see this in step 2 in the coefficients table in the regression printout above. You can also see in the model summary in the regression output that the total variance explained, R^2, became 32.6 percent.

Following the removal of the variance explained by both family life and work life, a third correlation is completed inside the regression procedure. This correlation is illustrated below in *Figure 68*.

Correlation Matrix

Pearson Correlations

		Anxiety	Worklife	Familylife	Res2
Anxiety	Pearson's r	—	0.715	−0.124	−0.042
	p-value	—	< .001	0.347	0.748
Worklife	Pearson's r		—	0.348	−0.000
	p-value		—	0.006	0.997
Familylife	Pearson's r			—	0.000
	p-value			—	0.999
Res2	Pearson's r				—
	p-value				—

Figure 68: Correlations with depression residuals after familylife and worklife covariance has been removed

Notice that both family life and work life have 0 correlation with these residuals. This makes perfect sense because the variance they shared with depression has already been explained, and removed.

Now, the procedure will look at the next variable to see if it explains a significant amount of the variance in these residuals. It does not. Almost all the variance anxiety explained has already been explained and removed from these residuals.

Because there is now no variable that explains a significant amount of variance in the residual variance, the procedure stops. Thus, the procedure revealed that two independent variables, family life and work life, explained 32.6 percent of the variance in depression.

BACKWARD and STEPWISE Regressions

The above regression procedure was a FORWARD Regression. A BACKWARD regression begins with all independent variables in the equation, and then checks to see if the independent variable that explains the least amount of unique variance is significant. It is significant if the amount of unique variance it explains in the dependent variable is a significant amount.

If that variable does explain a significant amount of variance then all variables in the equation are significant and all stay in, and the procedure stops. If that variable does not explain a significant amount of unique variance then it is removed and the same question is asked of the remaining variables until all variables explain a significant amount of variance.

A STEPWISE regression starts out like a FORWARD regression, but after each step there is a check of all variables in the equation to see if all that have entered still explain a significant amount of unique variance. At any time if there is a variable that fails this test, then it is removed from the equation.

If you do a study with only 3 independent variables, the result will likely be the same regardless of which type of entry procedure you choose. When there are several independent variables (only appropriate with larger sample sizes), BACKWARD regression will often result in the most variance explained, but it can also result with the variable that correlates most highly with the dependent variable left out of the equation.

FORWARD will always result in the variable that correlates most highly with the dependent variable in the equation (if any variables are significant). STEPWISE will often not explain as much variance as BACKWARD, and it can result in the variable that correlates highest with the dependent variable left out of the equation.

What do we report?

Multiple regression is most usually run to determine the amount of variance in the dependent variable (depression) that can be explained by the independent variables (family life, work life, and anxiety). It is also sometimes run to get a regression formula for prediction purposes, but as this is not normally the case, I will provide a results paragraph reporting variance explained. All the information for this paragraph is in the first two tables in the regression output (see *Figure 64*, above).

We wanted to determine the amount of variance in participants' depression scores that could be explained by their scores on family life, work life, and general anxiety. Therefore, we employed a forward selection multiple regression procedure. A significant amount of variance in depression was explained by family life and work life, but general anxiety failed to explain a significant amount of additional variance, $F(2,57) = 13.77$, $p<.05$. Family life explained 22.4% of the variance in depression scores, and work life explained an additional 10.2% of variance, resulting in a total of 32.6% of variance explained by these two variables. These results reveal that family life and work life are highly related to depression scores.

Because regressions are based on correlations, and because correlation relationships can either be causal or spurious we cannot say that the family life score and/or the work life score affected the depression score. We can only say that 32.6% of the variance in depression is explained by the family life and work life scores. One might say the language is pedantic in what can be said and in what cannot be said, but those are the rules. They are there for a good reason, and the language is pedantic.

Appendix 6: Assumptions tests

Normality

Metric variables must form a normal distribution. This does not apply to categorical or ordinal variables. There are statistical tests for normality but in many statistics packages, they do not take Ns into account, so normal variables can look significantly skewed due to the reduction in the $\underline{p}$ value that occurs with higher Ns. Because of this, it is recommended to use the following test. The required values can be obtained using Common/Descriptives/Descriptive statistics in JASP, then select skewness and kurtosis under statistics.

Z_{SKEWNESS}= SKEWNESS-0 / SE $_{\text{SKEWNESS}}$ and Z_{KURTOSIS}= KURTOSIS-0 / SE $_{\text{KURTOSIS}}$.

An absolute value of the score greater than 1.96 or lesser than -1.96 is significant at $P < 0.05$, while greater than 2.58 or lesser than -2.58 is significant at $P < 0.01$, and greater than 3.29 or lesser than -3.29 is significant at $P < 0.001$. In small samples, values greater or lesser than 1.96 are sufficient to establish normality of the data. However, in large samples (200 or more) with small standard errors, this criterion should be changed to $\pm$ 2.58 and in very large samples no criterion should be applied (that is, significance tests of skewness and kurtosis should not be used). (Ghasemi, & Zahediasl, 2012)

The test for normality helps ensure that significant results will not be missed. The t-test and the ANOVA are robust to violations to normality (Stonehouse & Forrester, 1998; Sawilowsky & Blair, 1992; Sullivan & d'Agostino, 1992). A variable that is not normal may sometimes be transformed into normality, and if not, a non-parametric test can be used with it.

With large sample sizes, you will not need to test for normality because practically every test is significant, so there is no concern about missing an important finding. If there is sufficient effect size to report, in large sample sizes you will always find significance, even if a metric variable is skewed or kurtotic.

Homogeneity of variances

Data compared from multiple groups should have the same variances. T-tests and ANOVAs are very robust regarding this assumption. If the assumption of homogeneity of variances is violated, the effect on the p value is very small. JASP will test for this assumption within t-tests and ANOVAs if you make that selection.

If variance from one group is significantly unequal to the variance of another group you will lose a very small amount of power, that is, you will have very slightly less chance of finding a significance both in a t-test (Brown & Forsythe, 1974) and in an ANOVA (Bathke, 2004).

If you have already found a significance (p is equal to or less than alpha) then you won't need to worry about it, because this assumption is to protect against the loss of power to find significance.

If you have just missed a significance you could run a non-parametric test, such as the Mann Whitney (a non-parametric test replacement for an independent t-test) to see if you can get a significance there. You would not be able to have a covariate in a non-parametric test, but if you randomly assign to treatment and control groups you still have a causal study.

It is unlikely that this violation will ever be a problem for you with real data from treatment and control groups.

Linearity

Data in a Pearson Correlation should have a linear relationship. When you look at a scatterplot revealing the relationship between two variables, if there is a curve in the path of the dots, then a Pearson Correlation will estimate the relationship between the two variables too low.

An Eta correlation will more accurately estimate the relationship between two variables that form a curvilinear relationship.

Independence

When separate groups are being tested, as in an independent t-test or in an ANOVA, no person can be in more than a single group, and the group members should not be matched.

Appendix 7: Data used in analyses

The data immediately below was used in all statistical tests other than for the reliability analysis and for the appendices examples. Data used in those are further below.

The data set below was used for:

Independent T-Test, page 60, and Paired t-tests, page 63

Running and reporting an ANOVA, page 66

Running and reporting an ANCOVA, page 68

Running and reporting a correlation, page 78

id	gend	trtm	pre	post
1	1	1	54	44
2	1	2	46	32
3	1	1	63	62
4	1	2	66	52
5	1	1	96	97
6	2	2	67	61
7	2	1	64	67
8	2	2	65	51
9	2	1	43	53
10	2	2	81	61
11	1	1	54	44
12	1	2	46	33
13	1	1	63	62
14	1	2	66	53
15	1	1	96	97
16	2	2	67	61
17	2	1	64	67
18	2	2	65	51
19	2	1	43	53
20	2	2	81	51

The following data was used for:

Running and reporting a reliability analysis, page 82

Appendix 1: An ANOVA with 3 means, page 131

Appendix 3: A repeated measures ANOVA with 3 means, page 143

It is generally recommended to have a higher N for reliability analyses.

Id	gender	trtm	pre	post	flwup	Item1	Item2	Item3	Item4	Item5
1	1	1	54	44	45	54	44	45	60	54
2	1	2	46	32	34	46	32	34	64	41
3	1	1	63	62	62	63	62	62	51	25
4	1	2	66	52	54	66	52	54	64	32
5	1	1	96	97	97	96	97	97	49	34
6	2	2	67	61	62	67	61	62	56	32
7	2	1	64	67	67	64	67	67	47	22
8	2	2	65	51	59	65	51	59	64	61
9	2	1	43	53	52	43	53	52	40	44
10	2	2	81	61	64	81	61	64	70	56
11	1	1	54	44	45	54	44	45	60	54
12	1	2	46	33	35	46	33	35	63	40
13	1	1	63	62	62	63	62	62	51	25
14	1	2	66	53	55	66	53	55	63	33
15	1	1	96	97	91	96	97	91	49	22
16	2	2	67	61	65	67	61	65	56	32
17	2	1	64	67	61	64	67	61	47	22
18	2	2	65	51	53	65	51	53	64	61
19	2	1	43	53	52	43	53	52	40	44
20	2	2	81	51	55	81	51	55	80	24
21	1	3	96	97	90	96	97	90	49	22
22	2	3	67	61	69	67	61	69	56	32
23	2	3	64	67	67	64	67	67	47	22
24	2	3	65	51	53	65	51	53	64	61
25	2	3	43	53	52	43	53	52	40	-1
26	2	3	81	61	64	81	61	64	70	56
27	1	3	54	44	45	54	44	45	60	54
28	1	3	46	33	35	46	33	35	63	40
29	1	3	63	62	62	63	62	62	51	25
30	1	3	66	53	55	66	53	55	63	49
31	1	1	54	44	45	54	44	45	60	54
32	1	2	46	32	34	46	32	34	64	41
33	1	1	63	62	62	63	62	62	51	25
34	1	2	66	52	54	66	52	54	64	45

35	1	1	96	97	97	96	97	97	49	22
36	2	2	67	61	62	67	61	62	56	32
37	2	1	64	67	67	64	67	67	47	22
38	2	2	65	51	53	65	51	53	64	61
39	2	1	43	53	52	43	53	52	40	43
40	2	2	81	61	64	81	61	64	70	56
41	1	1	54	44	45	54	44	45	60	54
42	1	2	46	33	35	46	33	35	63	40
43	1	1	63	62	62	63	62	62	51	25
44	1	2	66	53	55	66	53	55	63	34
45	1	1	96	97	91	96	97	91	49	22
46	2	2	67	61	68	67	61	68	56	32
47	2	1	64	67	67	64	67	67	47	22
48	2	2	65	51	53	65	51	53	64	61
49	2	1	43	53	52	43	53	52	40	44
50	2	2	81	51	55	81	51	55	80	24
51	1	3	96	97	91	96	97	91	49	22
52	2	3	67	61	62	67	61	62	56	32
53	2	3	64	67	67	64	67	67	47	22
54	2	3	65	51	53	65	51	53	64	61
55	2	3	43	53	52	43	53	52	40	44
56	2	3	81	61	64	81	61	64	70	56
57	1	3	54	44	45	54	44	45	60	54
58	1	3	46	33	35	46	33	35	63	40
59	1	3	63	62	69	63	62	69	51	25
60	1	3	66	53	55	66	53	55	63	44

The following data was used for:

Appendix 1: An ANOVA with 3 means, page 131

Appendix 2: An ANCOVA with 3 means, page 137

You do not have to include the residuals variable or the gender variable for these tests.

id	gen	trtm	pre	post	residuals
1	1	1	54	44	-4.482
2	1	2	46	32	-9.514
3	1	1	63	62	5.679
4	1	2	66	52	-6.934
5	1	1	96	97	11.936
6	2	2	67	61	1.195
7	2	1	64	67	9.808
8	2	2	65	51	-7.063
9	2	1	43	53	14.099
10	2	2	81	61	-10.999
11	1	1	54	44	-4.482
12	1	2	46	33	-8.514
13	1	1	63	62	5.679
14	1	2	66	53	-5.934
15	1	1	96	97	11.936
16	2	2	67	61	1.195
17	2	1	64	67	9.808
18	2	2	65	51	-7.063
19	2	1	43	53	14.099
20	2	3	81	51	-20.999
21	1	3	96	97	11.936
22	2	3	67	61	1.195
23	2	3	64	67	9.808
24	2	3	65	51	-7.063
25	2	3	43	53	14.099
26	2	3	81	61	-10.999
27	1	3	54	44	-4.482
28	1	3	46	33	-8.514
29	1	3	63	62	5.679
30	1	3	66	53	-5.934
31	1	1	54	44	-4.482
32	1	2	46	32	-9.514
33	1	1	63	62	5.679
34	1	2	66	52	-6.934
35	1	1	96	97	11.936

36	2	2	67	61	1.195
37	2	1	64	67	9.808
38	2	2	65	51	-7.063
39	2	1	43	53	14.099
40	2	2	81	61	-10.999
41	1	1	54	44	-4.482
42	1	2	46	33	-8.514
43	1	1	63	62	5.679
44	1	2	66	53	-5.934
45	1	1	96	97	11.936
46	2	2	67	61	1.195
47	2	1	64	67	9.808
48	2	2	65	51	-7.063
49	2	1	43	53	14.099
50	2	3	81	51	-20.999
51	1	3	96	97	11.936
52	2	3	67	61	1.195
53	2	3	64	67	9.808
54	2	3	65	51	-7.063
55	2	3	43	53	14.099
56	2	3	81	61	-10.999
57	1	3	54	44	-4.482
58	1	3	46	33	-8.514
59	1	3	63	62	5.679
60	1	3	66	53	-5.934

The following data was used for:

Appendix 4: A simple regression, page 151

Appendix 5: A multiple regression, page 155

id	trtm	pre	post	fwup	Anx	Wlf	Fmlf	Dep
1	1	54	44	45	54	45	45	54
2	2	46	32	34	44	33	36	41
3	1	63	62	62	63	62	49	25
4	2	66	52	54	44	54	36	32
5	1	96	97	97	96	97	51	34
6	2	67	61	62	67	62	44	32
7	1	64	67	67	64	66	53	22
8	2	65	51	59	65	59	36	61
9	1	43	53	52	43	52	60	44
10	2	81	61	64	81	63	30	56
11	1	54	44	45	54	45	40	54
12	2	46	33	35	40	35	37	40
13	1	63	62	62	63	62	49	25
14	2	66	53	55	66	55	37	33
15	1	96	97	91	96	91	51	22
16	2	67	61	65	67	65	44	32
17	1	64	67	61	64	61	53	22
18	2	65	51	53	65	52	36	61
19	1	43	53	52	43	51	60	44
20	2	81	51	55	81	55	20	24
21	3	96	97	90	96	90	51	22
22	3	67	61	69	67	69	44	32
23	3	64	67	67	64	66	53	22
24	3	65	51	53	65	53	36	61
25	3	43	53	52	43	52	60	-1
26	3	81	61	64	81	63	30	56
27	3	54	44	45	54	45	40	54
28	3	46	33	35	46	35	37	40
29	3	63	62	62	63	62	49	25
30	3	66	53	55	66	55	37	49
31	1	54	44	45	54	45	40	54
32	2	46	32	34	46	34	36	41
33	1	63	62	62	63	62	49	25
34	2	66	52	54	66	54	36	45
35	1	96	97	97	70	96	51	22
36	2	67	61	62	67	61	44	32
37	1	64	67	67	64	66	53	22

38	2	65	51	53	65	53	36	61
39	1	43	53	52	66	52	60	43
40	2	81	61	64	81	63	30	56
41	1	54	44	45	54	45	40	54
42	2	46	33	35	46	35	37	40
43	1	63	62	62	63	62	49	25
44	2	66	53	55	66	55	37	34
45	1	96	97	91	96	91	51	22
46	2	67	61	68	67	68	44	32
47	1	64	67	67	64	67	53	22
48	2	65	51	53	22	53	36	61
49	1	43	53	52	43	52	60	44
50	2	81	51	55	81	55	20	24
51	3	96	97	91	96	91	51	22
52	3	67	61	62	67	61	44	32
53	3	64	67	67	64	66	53	22
54	3	65	51	53	65	52	36	61
55	3	43	53	52	43	52	60	44
56	3	81	61	64	81	63	30	56
57	3	54	44	45	54	45	40	54
58	3	46	33	35	77	35	37	40
59	3	63	62	69	63	69	49	25
60	3	66	53	55	66	55	37	44

Appendix 8: Flowchart to pick a statistic

Purpose	variables	variables	Statistic
Determine level of relationship (correlations)	Metric	Metric	Pearson's
	Dichotomous	Metric	Run Pearson's, report a Point-biserial
	Dichotomous	Dichotomous	Run Pearson's, report a Phi Coefficient
	Ordinal	Metric	Spearman's Rho
	Ordinal	Ordinal	Spearman's Rho
	Dichotomous	Ordinal	Spearman's Rho
	Independent Variable (# and type) ↓	**Dependent Variable ↓**	
Predict or determine the amount of variance explained (regressions)	1 Metric	1 Metric	Simple Regression
	More than 1 Metric	1 Metric	Multiple Regression
Test to see if there is a significant difference	Testing frequency differences between levels of one variable		Chi Square Goodness of fit
	Testing for a frequency association between two variables		Chi Square Test of Association
	1 Dichotomous (independent)	1 Ordinal	Mann Whitney	Testing Ranks
	1 Dichotomous (repeated)	1 Ordinal	Wilcoxon	
	1 with >2 levels (independent)	1 Ordinal	Kruskal Wallis	
	1 with >2 levels (repeated)	1 Ordinal	Freidman's ANOVA	
(Significant difference tests that compare independent groups can be used in Causal Research Designs)	Dichotomous (independent) 2 means	1 Metric	Independent T-test	Testing Means
	Dichotomous (repeated) 2 means	1 Metric	Paired T-test	
	1 with 2 or more (independent) means	1 Metric	ANOVA	
	1 with 2 or more (independent) means while controlling for a covariate	1 Metric	ANCOVA	
	1 with 2 or more means from a single group (repeated)	1 Metric	Repeated Measures ANOVA	

References

American Psychological Association. (2010). Preparing manuscripts for publication in psychology journals: A guide for new authors. Washington, DC: Author.

American Psychiatric Association. (2013). Diagnostic and statistical manual of mental disorders (DSM-5®). American Psychiatric Pub.

Azar, B. (2006). Discussing your findings. American Psychological Association (APA). https://doi.org/10.1037/e451422006-009

Bartol, K. M. (1983). Manuscript faults and review board recommendations: Lethal and nonlethal errors. In American Psychological Association, Committee on Women in Psychology and Women's Programs Office, Understanding the manuscript review process: Increasing the participation of women (pp. 29–45). Washington, DC: American Psychological Association.

Bathke, A. (2004). The ANOVA F test can still be used in some balanced designs with unequal variances and nonnormal data. Journal of Statistical Planning and Inference, 126(2), 413-422. doi.org/10.1016/j.jspi.2003.09.010

Beck, A. T., Davis, D. D., & Freeman, A. (2015). Cognitive therapy of personality disorders. Guilford Publications.

Beck, A. T., Steer, R. A., & Brown, G. K. (1996). Beck depression inventory-II. San Antonio, 78(2), 490-8. https://doi.org/10.1037/t00742-000

Berrios, G. E. (1988). Melancholia and depression during the 19th century: a conceptual history. British Journal of Psychiatry, 153(3), 298-304. https://doi.org/10.1192/bjp.153.3.298

Brown, M. B., & Forsythe, A. B. (1974). Robust tests for the equality of variances. Journal of the American Statistical Association, 69(346), 364-367. https://doi.org/10.1080/01621459.1974.10482955

Burton, R., & Jackson, H. (1932). The anatomy of melancholy (Vol. 3). H. Jackson (Ed.). London: Dent.

Campbell, D. T., & Stanley, J. C. (1971). Experimental and Quasi-Exprimental Designs for Research (Vol. 4). Rand McNally.

Campbell, D. T., & Stanley, J. C. (2015). Experimental and quasi-experimental designs for research. Ravenio Books.

Ravenio Books. Cozolino, L. (2010). The neuroscience of psychotherapy: Healing the social brain. WW Norton & Company. https://doi.org/10.1177/036215371204200211

Dimitrov, D. M., & Rumrill Jr, P. D. (2003). Pretest-posttest designs and measurement of change. Work, 20(2), 159-165.

Emmerson, G. J., (2017). Sensory experience memory in Resource Therapy. International Journal of Clinical and Experimental Hypnosis, 65(1), 120-131. Doi: 10.1080/00207144.2017.1246882

Emmerson, G. J. (2016) The vivify specific induction: A resource therapy action. Australian Journal of Clinical Hypnotherapy and Hypnosis, 38(2), 19-25.

Emmerson, G. J. (2015). Learn Resource Therapy. Blackwood Victoria, Australia: Old Golden Point Press.

Emmerson, G. J. (2014a). Resource Therapy. Blackwood Victoria, Australia: Old Golden Point Press.

Emmerson, G. J. (2014b). Resource Therapy Primer. Blackwood Victoria, Australia: Old Golden Point Press.

Emmerson, Gordon J. (2004). The expression, removal and relief method of resolving trauma. Australian Journal of Clinical Hypnotherapy and Hypnosis, Vol 24(2), 121-139.

Ghasemi, A., & Zahediasl, S. (2012). Normality tests for statistical analysis: a guide for non-statisticians. International journal of endocrinology and metabolism, 10(2), 486-489. https://doi.org/10.5812/ijem.3505

Kielkiewicz, K., & Kennedy, I. (2015). Depression-Understanding and Therapeutic Intervention. Depression, 15(4).

Levine, T. R., & Hullett, C. R. (2002). Eta squared, partial eta squared, and misreporting of effect size in communication research. Human Communication Research, 28(4), 612-625. doi.org/10.1093/hcr/28.4.612

Rosenzweig, M. R., Love, W., & Bennett, E. L. (1968). Effects of a few hours a day of enriched experience on brain chemistry and brain weights. Physiology & Behavior, 3(6), 819-825. https://doi.org/10.1016/0031-9384(68)90161-3

Sawilowsky, S. S., & Blair, R. C. (1992). A more realistic look at the robustness and Type II error properties of the t test to departures from population normality. Psychological bulletin, 111(2), 352. https://doi.org/10.1037//0033-2909.111.2.352

Stonehouse, J. M., & Forrester, G. J. (1998). Robustness of the t and U tests under combined assumption violations. Journal of Applied Statistics, 25(1), 63-74. https://doi.org/10.1080/02664769823304

Sullivan, L. M., & d'Agostino, R. B. (1992). Robustness of the t test applied to data distorted from normality by floor effects. Journal of Dental Research, 71(12), 1938-1943. doi.org/10.1177/00220345920710121601

Trexler, Gitta Gertrud (1997) The analgesic effectiveness of hypnosis in the treatment of migraine and aura. PhD thesis, Victoria University of Technology.

Wang, Y. P., & Gorenstein, C. (2013). Psychometric properties of the Beck Depression Inventory-II: a comprehensive review. Revista Brasileira de Psiquiatria, 35(4), 416-431. https://doi.org/10.1590/1516-4446-2012-1048

Yurdugül, H. (2008). Minimum sample size for cronbach's coefficient alpha: A monte-carlo study. H. U. Journal of Education, 35, 397-405.

The author

Professor Gordon Emmerson specializes both in teaching therapy and in teaching research design and statistics. He currently presents workshops in both these areas across Australia and internationally. He has published numerous books and journal articles, and has coordinated university majors both in therapy and in social research.

Dr Emmerson is an Honorary Fellow in the School of Psychology at Victoria University, Melbourne. He is the author of the books 'Ego State Therapy' (2003, 2007, 2010), 'Advanced Techniques in Therapeutic Counseling (2006), Healthy Parts Happy Self (2012), Resource Therapy, (2014) Resource Therapy Primer (2014), Resource Therapy Trainer, (2015), and Learn Resource Therapy (2015). He developed Resource Personality Theory and Therapy and has developed techniques for working with many psychological conditions. As a registered psychologist and member of the Australian Psychological Society, he has published numerous refereed articles and has conducted and published experimental clinical research. Dr Emmerson has conducted workshops in Australia, South Africa, Germany, Switzerland, Austria, the UK, New Zealand, the US, and the Middle East. He makes keynote conference and convention addresses on his therapeutic approaches. He provides Foundation Training, a Clinical Qualification in Resource Therapy, Advanced Clinical Training in Resource Therapy, and Train the Trainer.

His upcoming Research Therapy workshops are listed at the URL, http://www.resourcetherapy.com. His research workshops may be found at http://acspri.com.au and http://www.nzssn.co.nz.

www.ingramcontent.com/pod-product-compliance
Lightning Source LLC
Chambersburg PA
CBHW051228290326
41931CB00039B/3285